THE EVENING SUN TURNED CRIMSON

Herbert E. Huncke

Introduction
by
Allen Ginsberg

Cherry Valley Editions

Cover design by Walter Hartmann.
Back cover photo by Louis Cartwright.

This book was made possible, in part, by funds from
The National Endowment for the Arts, a federal agency,
in Washington, D.C., and the New York State
Council on the Arts.

Typeset by The Open Studio Print Shop &
Design Center, Rhinebeck & Barrytown, N.Y.,
a non-profit facility for independent publishers &
individual artists, funded in part by grants from
The New York State Council on the Arts & The National
Endowment for the Arts.

Library of Congress Cataloging in Publication Data

Huncke, Herbert E.   1915-
     The evening sun turned crimson.

       1.   Huncke, Herbert E., 1915-   —Biography.
2.   Authors, American—20th century—Biography.
3.   Bohemianism—United States—Biography.
4.   Narcotic addicts—United States —Biography.
I.   Title.
PS3558.U466Z466   813'.5'4   79-2555
ISBN 0-916156-45-1
ISBN 0-916156-44-3 signed
ISBN 0-916156-43-5 pbk.

Cherry Valley Editions
Box 303
Cherry Valley, NY 13320

Contents

THE EVENING SUN TURNED CRIMSON

If universe is a dream-illusion as Gnostics & Buddhists chant, one Alien, one Stranger, one Caller of the Great Call, one Knower, one Enlightened Being waking in the midst of Dream can shiver the fundament of Kosmos with his lone realization—because it is the only verifiable thing among myriads of phantom phenomena.

> 'O go way Man I can
>   hypnotize this Nation
> I can shake the Earth's foundation
>   with the Maple Leaf Rag'

The whole stage-scenery of Moloch's altar-Time, Life, Fortune, Pentagon, Madison Avenue, Wall Street, Treasury Department, St. Patrick's Cathedral, Wrigley Building & all-shuddered evenescent in sunset, (The Evening The Sun Turned Crimson,) when Herbert E. Huncke's consciousness was opened.

Toward the end of the planetary conflict then called World War Two Mr. Huncke was a familiar stranger hustling around Times Square 42'nd Street New York, so Alien in fact that several years later the Police themselves banned him from the street as a Creep. A number of subtle revolutions had begun by that time: a change in national music to variable rhythmic base called Bop, a corresponding change in poetic Prosody (W. C. Williams' Variable American Foot), hip styles of diction & posture & hand-gesture signalling revolution of consciousness from Harlem & 52 Street jazz meccas, breakthroughs of cosmic consciousness (or planetary consciousness if the latter phrase is more acceptable to city-minded critics) occurring to Whitmanic isolatos in myriad cities of these States, drug-induced ecstasies & hallucinations passing from Black and Red subcultural hands into the heads of scholarly whites, changes in bodyawareness & recognition of sexual tenderness heretofore acknowledged by Sherwood Anderson in the same provincial American ken as prophet Walt Whitman. Herbert Huncke 7 on Times Square quite literally embodied all these hustling tendencies in his solitary frame, and was to be found in 1945 passing on subways from Harlem to Broadway scoring for drugs, music, incense, lovers, Benzedrine Inhalers, second story furniture, coffee, all night vigils in 42nd Street Horn & Hardart and Bickford Cafeterias, encountering curious & beautiful solitaries of New York dawn, in one season selling newspapers, in another serving as a connection for the venerable Dr. Alfred Kinsey pursuing his investigations of the sexual revolution statisticised for credibility, and in one Fall of the mid-Forties appearing as companion on the streets to Jack Kerouac, William Burroughs, myself and others.

Huncke's figure appears variously in Clellon Holmes' novel Go, there is an excellent early portrait in Kerouac's first Bildungroman The Town and The City, fugitive glimpses of Huncke as Gotham morphinist appear in William Lee's Junkie, Burroughs' dry first classic of prose. He walked on the snowbank docks with shoes full of blood into the middle of my own rhapsody, Howl, and is glimpsed in short sketches by Herb Gold, Carl Solomon & Irving Rosenthal scattered through subsequent decades.

As far as I know the ethos of what's charmingly Hip, & the first pronunciation of the word itself to my fellow ears, first came consciously from Huncke's lips; and the first information and ritual of the emergent hip subculture passed through Huncke's person. Not that he invented this style of late XX Century individualistic illumination & naked perception—but that in his anonymity & holy Creephood in New York he was the sensitive vehicle for a veritable new consciousness which spread through him to others sensitized by their dislocation from History and thence to entire generations of a nation renewing itself for fear of Apocalyptic Judgement. So in the grand Karma of robotic Civilizations it may be that the humblest, most afflicted, most persecuted, most suffering lowly junkie hustling some change in the all-night movie is the initiate of a Glory transcending his Nation's consciousness that will swiftly draw that Nation to its knees in tearful self-forgiveness.

One incidental condition of the junkie—Huncke in particular—should be understood (as it has not been in the mass hallucinations of Treasury Department propaganda multiplied millionfold by Collaborators such as The Readers Digest & The Daily News)—that the junk "Problem" as it exists circa 1970 is the result of a sadistic self-serving conspiracy by Narcotics Bureau & Mafia to perpetuate their own business, which is supervising the black market in Junk and selling Junk, which both groups conjoined have done for decades. Though the Supreme Court in its 1925 Lindner Decision specified that the original junkie-registration laws were not intended to prevent doctors from ethical maintenance treatment of junkies (as successfully practised with modifications to this day in Great Britain), agents of Government have illegally & forcibly blackmailed, trapped, propagandized, strong-armed & snowjobbed everybody in the socio-medical field of junkdom to impotent silence & political futility. Given this context, little know by the liberal public, Herbert Huncke coincides with Poe's old demonic dreaminess.

Like Anderson and like Poe, Huncke writes weird personal prose—provincial, awkwardly literate—the same characteristic exaggerated into insane rhetoric in Melville's Pierre makes that much unread book a funny delight to prose cognoscenti. Huncke's prose proceeds from his midnight mouth, that is, literal storytelling, just talking—for that reason it is both awkward and pure. There are traces of old hifalutin literary half-style that give a gentlemanly antiquity to the writer's character—Poe-esque or Chinese Moderne fustian of the Thirties & Prohibition. What is excellent as prose in The Evening Sun Turned Crimson is naked city man speech, clear and magnanimous as personal conversation. The book is memorable for these traces of American tongue, and equally remarkable for its chapters of American History.

ALLEN GINSBERG
September 18, 1968

9

THE EVENING SUN
TURNED CRIMSON

I remember so many strange happenings from the past sometimes I can sit after having taken a shot of heroin for several hours completely absorbed by visions of places and people and the odd twists which make one person or place or experience a bit outstanding from every ordinary routine.

Once when I was a young child I had been invited by friends of my parents to spend several weeks in the country living in a summer cabin as it was called—where there was a large flower garden and an even larger vegetable garden and great huge trees and hills and a beautiful winding river where I swam and went canoeing. There were narrow gravel roads twisting and climbing up and down hills—shaded on either side by old and gnarled trees where occasionally simply out of pure joy I would see one I could climb up into—sometimes reaching almost the very top branches which I would cling to swaying slightly from my own weight and while gazing out over the landscape I believed I could see for many miles and my whole body would delight at the softly blowing wind.

The people I lived with owned a big brown and white collie dog named Tamer and he was my constant companion. It was my first encounter with a dog as a friend and I talked to Tamer as though he could understand every thing I said—revealing secrets to him I had never shared with anyone.

The cabin or house was built at the top of a hill and from the screened enclosed front porch one could see clear over to the opposite side of the river. Immediately in front of the house the hill began descending and it was rather a long distance down to the river banks. In the evening the view of the setting sun was beautiful.

The one very unusual happening of that summer for me had to do with a sunset and all these years I've remembered every so often that particular sunset.

I was a fairly intelligent child and usually could be 11

depended upon to obey instructions and behave in a self reliant manner. Therefore when one afternoon I was left alone there was very little worry on the part of the people who had left me. I fail to recall why they had to leave me behind when they drove away but they had praised me and explained there was no need for me to have someone with me on this occasion since Tamer was to be left behind also and surely I was big enough to help myself to food which had been prepared and set aside for me and going to bed would be no problem. They assured me they would return before the next morning and of course I was too sensible a boy to be afraid of anything like the dark.

Actually I was thrilled at the prospect of having the house all to myself and reassured everyone that I was quite capable of taking care of myself. I think I was five years old at the time or perhaps six and extremely precocious.

And so suddenly I was all alone and master of the house. It was getting late in the afternoon and for the first time since I had come to this place I became aware of the sounds around me.

I had heard them before but not quite as I was hearing them now. Everything took on a new dimension for me and although everything was familiar—still there was seemingly something new about everything. I realized for the first time I was alone and I became a bit uneasy. It is rather difficult to explain now and was then but I had to admit to myself perhaps I wasn't very brave after all and this business of being alone was a good bit different than simply being indifferently aware of others being around or near.

I spoke to Tamer and kept him as near by as possible; even though I was still a long way from real fright it still felt good having him close. He and I moved through the several rooms of the cabin and although it wasn't dinner time I decided to have something to eat. There were only two neighbors and they had their places a good distance from our place and although I could look through the kitchen window and see another house through some trees—it seemed rather far away and again I was aware of being alone. I ate half heartedly and shared some of my food with Tamer and then decided to go and sit on the front porch and
watch the people below either rowing or paddling their

boats and canoes with every so often a small motor boat spreading a wake which would cause the other river craft to rock rather roughly and the people in the boats would break into smiles and the women invariably reached for the sides and their laughter sometimes carried up the side of the hill and could be heard by those of us watching from the security of our front porch.

On the evening of this story as I walked from the interior of the house out on to the porch I became aware of the sky which had turned a wild furious crimson from the huge glowing red disk of the sun radiating shafts of gold light and or at rushing speed plunged below the horizon. I stood—nearly rivited to the spot bathed in pinkish tint and surrounded by an almost red world—everything reflecting the sunset and filled with awe and an inward fright I felt the intenseness of my being alone and although I've suffered acute awareness of loneliness many many times throughout my life I've never sense it quite as thoroughly or traumatically as on that evening when all the world turned into burning flame and it was as though I was already in the process of being consumed. I was not brave at all any longer and was out and out afraid—plain scared—as I've ever been in my life.

Very slowly and carefully I looked all around me speaking in whispers to Tamer and finally along with Tamer withdrawing into the room which had been mine since my coming there to visit. I climbed into my bed and tried to coax Tamer up beside me. He simply refused and stalked in somewhat haughty manner out of the room disappearing from my view and eventually I suppose settling down for the night in his own spot.

There isn't much more except to say the sun setting on that warm summer evening was one of the most frightening experiences in my life. Today a sunset can fill me with an awareness of beauty that nothing else can.

BRIEF AUTOBIOGRAPHY

I was born in a small town in Massachusetts. Odd in a way because my father was born in Chicago and my mother in Laramie Wyoming and neither of them did any traveling until shortly before my birth. My father obtained work in a company manufacturing precision tools used around motor and machinery constructions. This was his chosen field and one he was respected in—later becoming something of an authority whose opinion was a decisive factor on several occasions among his associates concerning a point requiring the knowledge of an expert. At any rate going back to Greenfield Massachusetts in 1915 my parents and grand-mother—my mother's mother—were living there and I was on the way. My mother was quite young—fifteen and in ignorance of sex. My father was very nearly as bad al-though a few years older. At any rate he violated my mother in a rather crude fashion so the whole idea of sex became repellent (to her) and remained so until I was in my early teens and began opening her mind to a more honest ap-proach—later having the satisfaction of knowing she ac-cepted lovers and became better adjusted per result. This followed nearly twelve years of marriage with my father then two years of living separately and finally divorce.

I know my birth caused pain and fear and perhaps my mother never quite forgave me. We were friends but she always betrayed me and this became her way of balancing the score. She was truly a spoiled child who had wanted to sing and become part of the theater world and wasn't quite clear how she had become a wife and pregnant. I gathered later my grandmother was mostly responsible. She was a young wealthy widow and wanted to see a little of the world. My mother presented a bit of a problem and she presumably decided since my father was there—presentable and showed promise in his line—it was a good match.

My mother had also received generously from her father
14 and when the estate was settled had enough to help my

father establish himself finally in Chicago as an independent business man. My mother was having her first contact with the opposite sex. They made a good looking young couple and marriage was logical. All of it has never been quite clear in my mind and I speak of it from what I have heard from my mother my father and my grandmother.

My father was apparently going thru some kind of training period which lasted four years. I therefore spent my first four years in the New England town of my birth. We supposedly lived well and I have a very faint memory of a sled—some kind of fur coat and mittens—being drawn along thru a world of snow and ice finally reaching a little bridge festooned with icicles over a solidly frozen stream the banks piled high with snow and became afraid my father would let go of the rope and along with the sled I would slip off the bridge into the ice and snow below. This lack of trust in my father never changed.

There is another vague memory of Greenfield—having something to do with a wire basket I had climbed inside and tried rolling down a hill in. My mother came on the scene and whether or not I was punished I can't recall but I do remember her annoyance and her screaming at me.

The next positive memory occurred in Detroit where we lived for approximately a year and where my brother was born. I was playing on a porch—slipped and cut my head in such a way it was necessary to put stitches in the wound to close it. Also it must have been about then I developed a fear of fire engines and would run and hide under the bed whenever I would hear one roaring thru the streets.

Next there was Chicago and my real troubles began. Everything I did was wrong and what was supposed to be a substantial American middle class home was really a household of screaming hysterical women and an angry-confused and frustrated man. There was very little peace. My mother began unleashing her resentment of the injustices she felt were being perpetrated against her. There was no love and among the adults only nagging and arguing. At least one scene in which I recall my grandmother removing a pair of scissors from my mother's hands by force because she was threatening to cut her throat. There was much mystery 15 about my father's activities away from home. Other women —that type of thing. My mother always complaining—arguing first with my father then with my grandmother. My father became about this point openly hostile toward my grandmother allowing this attitude to grow over the years into intense hate.

Most of the love I was at all aware of came from my grandmother and I strongly resented anything which might lead to being separated from her. She indulged most of my whims and it was in her presence I could be myself. She was a very beautiful woman selfish and indifferent to things not affecting her directly. She had conditioned herself to believe she was entitled to and could get along with only what she considered the best. She spent fantastic amounts of money on clothes going only to the places money was the important factor. Elegant and expensive hotels—restaurants and living quarters. Much of this spilled over on to me and I have never quite lost my taste for the things money can buy. All in all she was never far away from us.

IN THE PARK

Morning—early—break of dawn—the sky clear and blue—the sun's rays reaching downward through the leaves and boughs of the trees outside our windows and bird calls prominent above the occasional voices of the early risers and the sounds from the stirring around of those just awakened. I have just returned from a long morning walk through the streets of the city. I have always enjoyed walking and much of my life has been spent roving city streets through the hours of darkness. Some of my more welcome memories and recollections have to do with my youth in Chicago and many-man-nights spent wandering through the city streets and parks and along the lake front finally resting atop a stone piling perhaps or on a bench watching the sun rise. I had adventures and strange experiences—frequently meeting and becoming involved with other night people. I learned much about sex and about the vast number of people who make up the so-called less desirable element in our American way of life. Haunted people—lonely people—misfits—outcasts—wanderers—those on the skids—drunkards—deviates of all kinds—hustlers of every description—male and female—old people and young people—and they came from every section of the country.

Were I requested to select the strangest—the most unusual—the most vicious—the most dangerous—generally the most outstanding—the saddest—the most frightening—the kindest—the one most in need of love—or the one most apt to give love—I would be completely stymied—and at this point—there are many I have forgotten. There is one—who stands out from the rest slightly—perhaps because—he was my first encounter with someone who was—according to even extreme comparison with what I had been taught was sane – beyond the limit and unboubtedly very sick and well along toward maniacal. He was—unquestionably an excellent example of just what can happen to a human being in a society geared to greed and power where the 17 human element is almost entirely ignored except in lip service to man as an individual—and which remains actively indifferent while spewing forth a constant mounting percentage of the population into the group known as—human waste—and is accounted for—by recognizing the tragedy as a sociological hazard to be excepted in the best of organized society.

I was about fourteen when I met him and although I was conscious of his aloneness it wasn't until considerably many more years were added to my age—I realized with any real degree of compassion—the stark horror he himself must have sensed almost constantly regarding his existence.

It was toward dusk of a warm late summer day—walking through a somewhat remote section of park—thickly wooded and little used by people out near the lake front—that I first became aware of him. I had left the path that wound around and through the area and was intending to make a short cut through the trees and bushes to the edge of the lake. I had just pushed through a heavy clump of bushes into a clearer area when I suddenly saw him standing a bit to one side up near the trunk of a large tree. He was partially facing toward me and as I rather abruptly halted—mostly because of being surprised by seeing him—he smiled—and said—"Hi." I answered—saying—"Hello—you kind of took me by surprise." While answering I looked at him more carefully—taking in his appearance in detail. He was thin and not much taller than me—with sharp pointed facial features and though his thin rather long mouth carried a smile—his eyes—light blue in color—remained cold and hard. His hair was dark blond—almost brown—straight and long—and part of it fell to one side of his face—covering his ear – and as I watched he raised his hand and pushed it back – only to have it again fall down as before. His hands were large – with exceedingly long fingers and somehow didn't seem to go with the rest of his appearance. He was wearing a white shirt—somewhat soiled and haphazardly tucked into his black trousers. He wore an old pair of badly scuffed brown shoes.

As I began moving intending to continue on my way—he stepped almost directly in front of me and reached out and took hold of my arm—up near the shoulder—and partly over the muscle. His long hard fingers dug into my flesh and as he applied pressure I winced with pain. He had taken me almost unaware and for a moment—I was as intensely frightened as I have ever been—my entire body seemed suffused with panic. I started to struggle—trying to break away. He exerted more force and for an instant I thought— he is going to kill me. He began speaking to me in a sort of imploring tone—begging me not to get scared—he wasn't going to hurt me—although he could—"See"—he said—and he raised one of his hands up toward my face—to show me—the gleaming blade of a knife. "I won't hurt you—come-on – over this way" – he said as he began half pulling me along with him toward some tall bushes.

By then—my fear and panic had subsided. Somehow seeing him up close had helped dispel some of the fear. He was younger than he had first appeared—probably some-where in his late twenties—and also—he had stirred my curiosity in some fashion.

I can't remember all that transpired in the short dis-tance we covered but I had started talking and had suc-ceeded in establishing a sort of friendly note into the situation so that as we reached the bushes—he removed his hand from my arm and although he still carried his knife—he seemed less menacing.

It was still quite light and, although the whole area was filled with shadows, one could see plainly.

We pushed into the bushes—stooping over a bit to avoid being scratched on the face—with me in the lead. There was a clear space in the center and we stopped. It became obvious to me immediately that he had been there before. Lying on the ground was a black jacket folded—and leather briefcase. He told me to sit down and as I did he squatted down in front of me for a moment then sank down to a sitting position on the ground—his legs stretched out in front of him. He was in a position where—although he was in front of me—I was facing his side. He fumbled in his shirt pocket and found a couple of cigarettes—one of which he gave me. Putting his knife down somewhere along his side away from me he located matches and lighted our cigarettes. He allowed himself to lean back a little and drew deeply on his smoke. We had both been quiet while this had 19 taken place and I was a bit startled when he threw his cigarette down suddenly and said—"Look at that—ever see anything like it"—and he reached down to the fly of his pants—pulled it open and drew out his cock. It was enormous. "Bet you never saw one that big before"—he said as he began slowly masturbating. He was quite right—I had never seen anything—even remotely comparable in size or length and my thought was—that he was some kind of freak of nature and that this was some kind of malformation.

"You're a nice kid"—he said. "I think you wouldn't laugh at someone—who is different—just because they are different. Here—put your hand on my cock. Just hold it—don't move it—but squeeze—not too hard—just squeeze. I want you to see some pictures."

I reached over and held his cock in my hand—complying with his request. He picked up his briefcase—opened it and began removing stacks of photographs. He put them down by his side and then putting the briefcase out of the way—he picked up one of the photographs and showed it to me. It was the picture of a little girl maybe seven or eight years old completely nude. Looking at it more closely I saw where pencil marks had been drawn around the small mound of her pussy to look like hair. "Ain't she a little doll"—he said. "Do you think I could stick this into her?" And pushing my hand away he grabbed his cock in his hand and furiously jerket it for a minute or two all the time muttering obscene words—half stuttering out statements—about how good it would feel and about it being best and a favor to a girl to get fucked young and especially with a big cock because then later—no other cock unless bigger could ever hurt her. He threw down the first picture and began picking up one after another—showing them to me. Most were of children and many were of children without clothing. In one there was a little boy and little girl and apparently he disliked the idea of the little boy having a penis because he had blotted it out with black ink. There were several of naked women and he described in detail how thrilled they would be if he were to fuck them. Finally he returned to the first picture. This apparently was his favorite and he gazed at it almost tenderly. All the time he had continued playing with himself 20 and now he reached over and began fumbling with me. The whole experience had been unnerving and I hadn't had an erection but as he opened my trousers and began playing with me I grew excited. He looked at my cock closely—making little comments about my never comparing to him—and that I would never save some little girl from being hurt. He stopped playing with me—telling me to begin jerking myself so he could watch. As I began he aplied himself more vigorously to his own masturbation—all the time talking about fucking the little girl. "I got it in her now—oh it feels good—it's way up in her belly—I've got my big prick in her little tight cunt—it's in up to the balls—oh it's good—I'm going to come in her—I'm getting ready—oh I feel it coming—all my hot juice is for her—oh watch." With that he ejaculated—over and over again—his whole body shaking and quivering and as he slackened up—he started weeping.

BRIEF AUTOBIOGRAPHY II

Yet in a sense up till then the world had been my oyster and if I can recall any happiness in my childhood it will in all probability have to do with other persons than my parents— or with some adventure of my own.

Maybe with my grandmother who loved me with a love I believed in—even at this date—aware it was the only honest love I knew as a child. Grams accepted me. I could dance in front of her—twisting—turning—trying to spin all in an effort to become like the music filling the room from the victrola I never grew tired of listening to—and she would know and I could throw my arms around her when the music stopped and she would gather me laughing and exclaiming about my loss of breath—sometimes she would tell me stories of the West when she was a young girl—and speak of Indians or Billy the Kid—and of camping trips up into the Rocky Mountains describing mountain streams old and clear rushing downward—of wild flowers—of hunt- ing mountain lions and bears—of ranch life or of my grand- father I've never known who died before I was born—who when alive rode horseback—and owned thousands of heads of cattle—and made money speculating in the cattle buying markets—selling out at great profit and how he had given my mother a pony when she was about my age. She had loved her years in the West and there was a feeling of pride concerning the good and the bad she had seen or lived thru. She and I secretly knew I could be a great cowboy—ride a horse—toss a lariat—live out West—but that I'd probably spend most of my life stuck in Chicago. She enjoyed taking me along with her when she had shopping to do or perhaps simply wanted to have lunch in some good restaurant—and I enjoyed going along. I didn't mind wearing my good clothes and using good table manners—I always knew there would be some new kind of food to try or maybe I could have what was called a club sandwich and without fail – ice cream or

some pastry I'd never tried. We got on well together—she

would perhaps comment on the place and frequently of the people around us—or most often of the plans for my future and some of the things she would sometime want to do for me. I was perfectly comfortable and stimulated by the people and maybe simply by the idea of eating in a restaurant. I would really be thrilled if we had gone somewhere they used luncheon music as an added attraction. We loved each other and were happy together but my father resented the idea—telling her—she was making a god damned sissy out of me—to leave me alone. She would draw herself up very proudly and bend forward to kiss me—telling me to run along and play elsewhere—my father was tired and didn't mean what he had said. So with my grandmother there was some happiness other than that I stumbled on in the world away from home.

Much of what I have spoken was during the twenties. My mother cut her waist length golden hair one day in exchange for a hair style called a bob and a shingle. The change startled the older members of the family far more than me although to this day I remember her sitting in front of her dresser brushing so many strokes of her brush through her gold colored hair. Skirts were short—frequently above the knee. My mother loved them because they displayed well shaped legs. My parents were examples of the young smart set. They drank gin and smuggled whiskey. My father paid his bootlegger once a month and referred to the transaction as an account. They were entertained frequently and did much entertaining of their own. The people they knew as friends were usually in the age group of middle to late twenties for the men. The women were apt to be younger in their early twenties. The men were mostly in business for themselves and making money rapidly. They belonged to a country club and played golf on weekends. The women joined bridge clubs and played bridge at least two afternoons a week for money. They drank all afternoon when they were playing and I can hear the chatter amid the laughing I would walk in upon after school when it was my mother's turn to have the club at her home. Women were driving cars of their own—my mother's best friend had just received a new car as a gift from her husband and she and my mother made use of that car. My parents prided them- 23 selves on being modern. They all had the whole world in their pockets and it lasted about nine years—for some and for many only a few years longer and for the remaining it never changed although the pace certainly slowed down to a near stop but not quite. All of a sudden everything was in turmoil—stock market crash—well known names linked to suicide—swindles—underhanded deals. Talk about loss of fortunes overnight—the millionaires being hit. Small business men were hurt also—but the majority—like my father —had good solid backing and only had to hold on until the financial world made some readjustments. All would be well. Unfortunately for thousands upon thousands of people everywhere—the only changes were progressively worse— until at last there was hunger and extreme deprivation. People couldn't work because there was no work. Bank savings had been lost—many banks went under and closed. There was talk about depression. Finally Roosevelt was elected and the government began projects to help relieve conditions—Works Projects—Conservation Camps—etc. The country slowly began coming alive again with a whole set of new rules.

My father had borrowed heavily from my grandmother to keep his business going—signed notes he several years later stole back and destroyed refusing to repay any of the loan. A short while following the market crash—my parents decided they would be wiser to split—the first move to be a period of separation. Our large apartment was given up and my brother, my mother, my grandmother and myself moved into a smaller so-called efficiency apartment in a first class middle class neighborhood. It was not a great distance from where we had been living and I was to continue attending the same school. On the way home—my first day—I met a brother and sister who lived on the same street I did in a lake front building and why didn't I come on to their place after checking in at home—we could fool around on the beach. The boy's name was John or Johnie and he was twelve—a year older than his sister whose name was Donna—who became my first love—the first girl that I kissed. I was the same age as Donna and we sort of permitted John to take over the responsibility of finding things for us to do. Their
24 parents were divorced and they were living with their mother

also and this gave us a common bond. We three became inseparable for the next seven or eight years. The three of us were rather wild. We began smoking immediately and I did it openly before my mother, offering her a choice of that or not seeing but knowing I was sneaking around doing it anyway. She became reconciled to the idea accepting it as part of the new values she had just started to acquire. As a disciplinarian my mother was completely ineffectual and from that point on I was almost entirely on my own and came and went as I chose. There were certain rules in the beginning I had to accept but it was only about a year or two later when there were no more rules and I did exactly as I pleased. I had along with John and Donna turned on a little gin we had stolen from a bottle belonging to his mother. We had felt rather exhilarated and considered ourselves pretty wise. We spent much time going to movies and talking about sex and resenting school and telling each other we would avoid all the stupidities of parents. Johnie had always been deeply attached to his mother and it was mostly because of this I tried reaching my mother a little more honestly and met with luck. I was startled to realize how much more about sex and the world I was aware of than she. She was lonely and upon discovering I was no little boy but someone she could talk to—she began talking. She was a romantic and up to this point refused to accept the fact the world was real and there was such a thing as sex and it was not necessarily bad or evil. She had never once in her life acknowledged the truth. There had never been any warmth in her relationship with her mother nor for that matter could either of them be honest with the other. My grandmother was way beyond my mother in worldly knowledge but peculiarly enough simply could not tell her own daughter a few basic facts. I decided I would try and help my mother to become a woman. It wound up I succeeded fairly well—by then I had been abused by her—my trust never once kept—betrayed systematically— screamed and cursed at—my most vulnerable spots deliberately revealed—lied about and to—yet there were times we actually communicated and today I can look back on our relationship and recall only the pleasant and funny aspects. She was as much a victim as anyone could be and 25 until my concern defenseless. She would have in all probability ended up in a mental institution.

We remained in our new surroundings a little over a year—when my parents decided to live together again—this time selecting an entirely new part of the city to set up their new home in. Same type neighborhood as always—but a little sharper location closer to the heart of the city. I liked it considerably better. They selected a comfortable apartment and started a routine which finally ended a year later in the divorce court. My mother was to keep the apartment and have custody of her children—my brother and myself—and to receive two hundred and fifty dollars every month from my father for the upkeep of the home and our maintenance. A beautiful deal until my father began feeling the pressure and started seeking a way to get out from under. My grandmother's money had started running out and she requested payment on one of the notes—a sum of three or four thousand dollars. He hit the ceiling—he couldn't do it at the moment—she would have to wait.

Johnie and Donna had talked their mother into moving into a place less than two blocks away. Again we were constant companions—older and wiser—less innocently amused than before. Donna dated an outside acquaintance—occasionally preferred being with Johnie and me.

I was passably good looking with an abundance of sex appeal. I started ejaculating about eleven and since had been having sex steadily of all kinds. I had played around with and laid a young girl I met at school—not once but many times. I had run across a strange character with a canoe he would carry down to the lake shore and then paddle out to one of the breakwaters off shore—there he would take his clothes off lying naked in the sun for hours. He took me along when I first met him and as soon as our clothes were off he began sucking me off—it was one of the wildest sensations I had ever known. Sometimes I would wait for him. I liked head and let him give it to me as frequently as it could be arranged. I introduced Johnie to him and as often as not Johnie would go along with me.

At about this time Donna was sent to a Catholic school where she withdrew to some extent from Johnie and me. While in school she became friends with a beautiful young girl from Kansas. When vacation time arrived Donna was invited to spend several weeks in Kansas. She accepted the invitation. When she returned she was hopelessly in love with the girl and believed herself definitely a lesbian. I had but recently discovered the whole homosexual scene and was entirely sympathetic to her feelings. We spent many hours—just the two of us—shutting her brother out for the first time—talking and discussing the possibilities of the future. This was in fact the beginning of a period of time filled with happenings and experiences I can't possibly hope to recall in chronological order. The three of us became well known and moved thru and in and out of many scenes taking place. Donna changed lovers rapidly and had started drinking heavily. There were parties lasting many days. People drinking themselves drunk and sober again. Occasionally someone would suddenly fall out flat and would be picked up—placed somewhere and left to sleep it off while the party ground out to the end. There was an air of desperation about the people involved in these routines as they were deliberately seeking self destruction. They were on the whole beautiful people in appearance but filled with anger and hate. Love was spoken of and declared but seldom meant more than the sex involved. The large gatherings of lesbians invariably revealed the women in their most obnoxious displays. Screaming kicking and biting—threatening each other—stealing lovers—engendering huge seething scenes aflame with jealousy and ugliness. Frequently Johnie and myself would be the only males present. Johnie was accepted with liking and far more respect than I was and most of the time had it not been for him and his sister I wouldn't have been around at all. It was shortly prior to the repeal of prohibition and beer flats were popular. These were apartments where beer and whiskey was sold. Frequently poker games would be in progress and some of the games would get hot with several hundred dollars in the pot. Usually it was the more masculine types that played and they were at their best. Many were good players and enjoyed themselves. Many had girls out on the streets hustling. The girls would begin returning around two or three in the morning and were ready to start a little steady drinking. Once or twice a few had fallen in with pot or tea as 27 it was called then and I picked up for the first time one morning and got so stoned I was unable to move. It was up to then the most unusual and soul conscious experience of my life. I heard music for the first time – that is really heard it – saw people I had known in a whole new perspective becoming aware of entirely new levels of consciousness. I was entranced and on the spot became a confirmed smoker. It is great, great stuff and should be smoked by everyone. I have had three or four soul shattering encounters with other things but nothing has ever delighted me quite as much as my first high on pot. No matter what I have been doing or where I might be at the time smoking pot is sure to have enriched the moment.

I discovered where pot was easily obtained and copped steadily from then on. It was very cheap and I could pick up a Prince Albert Tobacco can packed full for one dollar or at most one dollar and a half. Sometimes I'd buy five or six sticks for twenty-five cents.

FIRST LOVE

When I was a schoolboy—age 15—living in what was conceded to be a respectable middle class neighborhood in Chicago I had my first encounter with love.

In the apartment building in which I lived with my mother, brother and grandmother there were several women who owned Chow dogs and they would pay me to take their dogs out for walks. This afforded me opportunity to make something of a show of myself—since Chows were quite fashionable—and as I considered myself at least personable in appearance it rather pleased me to imagine that people seeing me walking along the Drive must surely think me the owner and certainly attractive with my pet straining at the leash. Frequently I would walk one of the dogs late in the evening and it was on such an occasion I first met Dick.

I had decided before returning home to stop by the neighborhood drugstore and as I was leaving someone spoke my name. I looked up into the most piercing brown—almost black brown—eyes I have ever seen. They belonged to a man who at the time was in his late 20s—fairly well built—not too tall—with somewhat aquiline features and exceedingly black hair which he wore combed flat to his head. I learned later he was of Russian Jewish parentage.

I was very much impressed by his appearance and felt a strange sensation upon first seeing him which was to be repeated each time we met for as long as I knew him. I never quite got over a certain physical response to his personality and even now in retrospect I find myself conscious of an inner warmth.

As I was leaving the drugstore, after he had spoken my name and I had smiled and flushed, he commented that I didn't know him but that a friend of his had spoken with me one evening about my dog and that I had given him my name and he in turn had given it to him when they had seen me walking and he had asked if his friend noticed me. He then asked me if I would object to his accompanying me home so that we might become better acquainted. He gave me to understand that he wanted to know me. I was no end pleased by his attention and became animated and flirtatious.

We had a thoroughly enjoyable walk and from that point on I began seeing him fairly regularly. He was in the recording business and was second in charge of a floor of recording studios in one of the large well known office buildings just off Lake Shore Drive a short distance north of the Loop. He knew innumerable people in show business and I spent as much time hanging around the studios as could be arranged. Sometimes we would lunch together or stay downtown for dinner or go to a movie or he would take me along while he interviewed some possible recording star and it was after some such instance at the old Sherman Hotel that he suggested since it was late I call home and ask permission to spend the night downtown. This I was anxious to do as I had long had the desire to sleep with him.

I was still rather green as to what was expected in a homosexual relationship but I did know I was exceedingly desirous of feeling his body near mine and was sure I could be ingenious enough sexually to make him happy with me.

Actually I had but little experience other than mutual masturbation with others of my own age and although I knew the word homosexual I wasn't exactly aware of the connotations.

We spent the night together and I discovered that in fact he was nearly as ignorant as I and besides was filled with all sorts of feelings of guilt. We kissed and explored each other's body with our hands and after both ejaculating fell asleep in each other's arms.

This began a long period in which he professed deep love for me and on one occasion threatened to throw acid in my face should he ever discover me with someone else.

The affair followed the usual pattern such affairs follow and after the novelty wore off I became somewhat bored although it appeased my vanity to feel I had someone so completely in my control. Had anyone threatened my supremacy I would have gone to great lengths to eliminate them from the situation.

About this time it was necessary for him to make a business trip to New York and when he returned he was wearing a Persian Sapphire ring which he explained he would give me if I would promise to stay away from some of the people and places I had lately been visiting. I promised to do this and considered the ring mine.

One evening we had dinner in a little French restaurant we frequented and while eating a very handsome young man joined us who Dick introduced as Richard who was attending classes at the University of Chicago and was someone he had met recently thru some mutual acquaintance. We sat talking and suddenly I was startled to see the ring on Richard's finger.

Richard was considerably younger than Dick and really very beautiful. He was blond with icy blue eyes—innocent and clear. He was very interested in life and people and kept bombarding us with questions—about our interests, the theater, music, art or whatever happened to pop into his head. He laughed a great deal and one could feel a sense of goodness about him. He was obviously attracted to me and asked permission to call me on the phone so that we might make arrangements to see each other. I complied and began making plans about how to get the ring away from him—after all I felt the ring was mine—and I wanted it.

And so it happened that I succeeded in twisting one of the few really wonderful things that occurred when I was young into a shame.

As I have already said Richard was good. There was no guile in his makeup and he offered his love and friendship unstintingly. It was he who first introduced me to poetry—to great music—to the beauty of the world and who was concerned with my wants and happiness. Who spent hours making love to me caressing and kissing me on every part of my body until I would collapse in a great explosion of beauty and sensation which I have never attained in exactly the same way with anyone since. He truly loved me and asked nothing in return but that I accept him instead of which I delighted in hurting him and making him suffer in all manner of petty ways. I would 31 tease him or refuse him sex or call him a fool or say that I didn't want to see him. Sometimes I would tell him we were finished, thru, and not to call me and try and see me and it was after one such episode on a beautiful warm summer night when I had agreed to see him again if he would grant me a favor—I asked for the ring and he gave it to me.

The next day I visited Dick at the studios and with many gestures and words of denunciation—flung the ring at him, telling him that we were finished and that anyway he wasn't nearly as amusing as Richard and that maybe and maybe not I'd continue seeing Richard but that in fact he bored me and I only felt sorry for him—and I would never be as big a fool over anyone as he was over me—and besides my only reason for knowing him at all was so that I could get the ring.

Dick became enraged and began calling me foul names which he sort of spit at me and pulled from his desk drawer a pistol. He was waving it in front of my face and at the same time telling me how cruel and heartless I was and that he could forgive the stupidity of my actions in regard to himself but that the harm I was inflicting on Richard was more than he could stomach and that I would be better dead. Suddenly he started shouting—"get out— get out—I never want to see you again." By this time I was shaking and almost unable to stand and stumbled out of his presence.

The following day in the mail I received a letter from Richard containing a poem—that read almost like this—

> A perfect fool you called me.
> Perchance not as happy in my
>   outlook on life and people
>   as you—
> Yet in like manner—playing the
>   role of a perfect fool—
> Gave me a sort of bliss—
> You in all your wisdom—will never know.

Shortly after receiving the letter I called Richard and asked to see him. He refused to see me and at that time I would not plead. A strange thing had happened to me—I had become aware—almost overnight—of the enormity of my cruelty and I was filled with a sudden sense of loneliness— which I have never lost—and I wanted Richard's forgiveness.

Richard never forgave me and I have only seen him once since the time he gave me the ring and that was only long enough for him to tell me—he was trying to forget he had known me. It was a cold winter day.

Nor did I ever speak with Dick again. Not so many years ago—I read in the paper—he is dead.

NEW ORLEANS 1938

I recall a night in New Orleans on St. Charles Street—walking. It had been raining—the streets were glistening—pools of rainwater reflected the night. Sound of drops of water dropping and spattering on the leaves of the magnolia trees. The streets were deserted—only an occasional passing automobile. I was crossing a side street when as I glanced up I saw a man approaching. He was about my own height. He was of stocky build inclined a bit toward fat—wearing dark trousers and a white shirt open three buttons at the neck—exposing a heavy growth of black hair. His complexion was swarthy—his eyes were small and dark brown. His hair was black and oily which he wore combed back straight from his forehead. His hands were in his pockets—a dangling cigarette hung from the corner of his mouth. Slightly lurching toward me—he asked for a match.

As I gave him a light for his cigarette he stood in front of me—wavering—sort of off balance—placing his hands on my shoulder—squinting his eyes—staring into my face—saying—"You look like a nice guy. I bet a person's color doesn't make any difference to you. Want a drink?—Come on—I'll buy you a drink."

I was strictly on the bum—any situation had—so to speak—to be taken advantage of—also I was curious about the man.

We turned off St. Charles Street—walking in the direction of I believe—South Rampart Street—near a railway depot. Reaching Rampart Street—we entered a Saloon—almost the first we encountered. The interior was lighted by a single unshaded light bulb hanging suspended in the center of the room. A large neon trimmed Juke Box occupied space along one wall. Several tables surrounded by straight back chairs were placed around the room—at one slouched a dark skinned negro—wearing blue denim overalls—his arms and hands hanging limp toward the floor—his head resting on the table top. At the bar—which was painted bright orange—two men stood talking. A record with a lot of horns and beating drum was on the Juke Box.

We stood at the bar drinking wine. The man was telling me something about cockroaches. He kept saying—"never kill a cockroach—never kill a cockroach." Several were walking around the spots of spilled wine and beer—waving their antennas. Suddenly he said he wanted to get laid. "Let's go and find a bar where there are some women—Come on—I know where one is. It's not far—just around the corner."

We departed walking along Rampart Street for about two blocks. The street was bare—lined solidly on either side with stores. One street light shone dimly—set high up on a pole—two men were walking—hands in their pockets—talking—hurrying—just out of the glow. We turned down a side street a short distance—into a store—the glass windows —painted black on the bottom halves. Inside—another un-shaded light bulb—a few tables—no Juke Box but a number of people—some standing at a short bar of unpainted lumber. A few were women—rather bedraggled appearing—none young—clothing rather shapeless—hanging askew. They were speaking almost shrilly moving around—laughing watching everything with their eyes. One came slightly stumbling toward us—carrying a wine glass—saying—"Is you going to buy me a drink—Honey?" She was thin—not young—her hair sticking out in stiff wisps from beneath a black hat. She was short in stature—light brown in color— with small facial features—her mouth narrow—open showing bad teeth—two or three missing in front.

The man—bought her a drink. They began talking— joking lasciviously at one another. He asked her what she charged for a lay. She said—"a dollar—I'se a good lay, mister—I'll show you a good time." He replied—all he had was seventy-five cents—and he wanted me to go along and watch. She agreed. She led us out of the bar room down the street to a small brick building—set back a small space— from the street—lighted inside the hallway at the top of a flight of stairs—by a gas-jet flame—into a room—just off the top of the stairs—holding a large brass bed—a dresser and mirror with a kerosene lamp burning—sitting on the surface in front of the mirror—a straight back chair and a small table—a large white crockery pitcher—a bowl set on 35 top of a bedside stand.

Without removing her hat she flopped backward on the bed—pulling her skirts up around her waist. He approached her clumsily—finally lowering his weight down on her—his pants part way down to his knees. They began squirming and panting. She began repeating obscenities—supposedly to excite him—interspersing remarks about him being good also saying—"Come on daddy—oh daddy—you'se good— you make baby feel good" moving more rapidly and frantically. This lasted a long while—until perspiration was rolling down their faces making a squelchy sound as they would come together.

Suddenly he stopped—arose from her—mopping his face with a handkerchief—then fumblingly pulling on his pants—saying—"I ain't going to pay you—nothing happened —you ain't any good." She stood up—her clothing half falling into place as she sort of tugged at it—saying—"please mister—I did the best I could—it's hot—You been drinking— please white man—I needs the money—a half dollar—that's half—a quarter so I can buy a drink."

I had been sitting. He motioned for me to leave ahead of him. As I walked thru the door he followed close behind. We moved rapidly down the stairs—back out to the street in the general direction of St. Charles Street. Reaching a better lighted area—we stopped—saying goodnight. He gave me a dollar just before he stumbled away—disappearing into the night. I never knew whether he gave the woman any money or not.

TATOOED MAN

Mardi Gras just passed in New Orleans—thinking about it recalls to mind Don Castle the tattooed man—I had met one evening on Oak St. Beach in Chicago – later running into him in New Orleans. He was a rather strange man – an ex-junky-freak show worker and poet—tattooed from a line circling his neck—like a collar—to his wrists on both arms and his ankles on both legs. There was a large red rose tattooed on his penis—he delighted telling about—describing in detail the discomfort and pain he had suffered at the time of the actual tattooing. He lived alone and claimed kindredship with spirits from another world. He was something of a mystic—talking hours on end about God—what God is—what God wants for mankind and how after death God absorbs into his being—representative of central life force—the entity we know as ourselves. He said that he had seen God and talked with him.

He was a lonely man and often spoke longingly of his days as the tattooed man—in a side show—when he knew the india-rubber man—the fat woman—the bearded lady—the sword swallower—the snake charmer—geeks—midgets —circus people—roustabouts—clowns—animal trainers—tight rope walkers—trapeze artists all kinds of people connected with side shows and big tops. For some reason he had gotten away from all that—no longer in touch with the only element he felt comfortable in. He was vague about what had happened but I gathered—from conversational bits—he had started using junk—finally getting hooked and eventually having a run in with the police—having served time. At any rate he felt he could no longer go back.

ELSIE

Sometimes I remember Chicago—and my experiences while growing up and as a youth. I remember in particular the people I knew and as frequently happens, I think, with people I associate whole periods of time as indicative of certain changes within myself. But mostly I think about the people and I recall one person rather vividly not only because he was obviously out of the ordinary but because I recognize now, what a truly beautiful creature he was.

He was a giant—well over six and one half feet tall with a large egg shaped head. His eyes were enormous and a very deep sea blue with a hidden expression of sadness as though contemplating the tragedy of his life as irrevocable. Also there were times when they appeared gay and sparkling and full of great understanding. They were alive eyes always and had seen much and were ever questing. His hair was an exquisite shade of henna red which he wore quite long like a woman's. He gave it special care and I can see it reflecting the light from an overhead bulb which hung shadeless in the center of his room while he sat crosslegged in the center of a big brass bed fondling his three toy pekes who were his constant companions and received greatly of his love. His body was huge with long arms which ended with thin hands and long tapering fingers whose nails were sometimes silver or green or scarlet. His mouth was large and held at all times a slightly idiot smile and was always painted bright red. He shaded his eyelids green or blue and beaded the lashes with mascara until often they were a good three quarters of an inch long. He exhibited himself among freaks in sideshows as the only true hermaphrodite in human life and called himself Elsie-John. When I met him he was in his early thirties.

He came originally from somewhere in Germany and before coming to this country had traveled—travailed if you prefer—much of Europe and could talk for hours of strange experiences he'd had. He was a user of drugs and although he liked cocaine best he would shoot up huge amounts of heroin afterward sitting still like a big brooding idol.

When I first knew him he was living in a little theatrical hotel on North State Street. It was an old hotel and in all probability is no longer in existence. Apparently at one time it had been a sort of hangout for vaudeville actors. It was shabby and rundown and the rooms were small and in need of fresh paint. He lived in one of these rooms with his three dogs and a big wardrobe trunk. One of the things I remember distinctly was his standing in front of a long thin mirror which hung on the wall opposite his bed—applying make-up—carefully working in the powder bases and various cosmetics creating the mask which he was seldom without.

When I met him I was coming out of a Lesbian joint with a couple of friends and upon seeing him for the first time was sort of struck dumb. He was so big and strange. It happened that one of the girls knew him and he invited us all up to his room to smoke pot—tea it was called in those days. His voice was rather low and pleasant with a slight accent which gave everything he said a meaning of its own. When we were leaving he suggested I come back and it was not much time until I became a constant visitor and something of a friend.

He liked being called Elsie and later when I introduced him—it was always as Elsie.

We began using junk together and sometimes I would lie around his place for two or three days. A friend of mine called John—who later was shot to death by narcotic bulls in a hotel while making a junk delivery—they grabbed him as he was handing the stuff over and he broke free and ran down the hall and they shot him—joined us and we became a sort of threesome.

Elsie was working an arcade show on West Madison Street and though junk was much cheaper then than now he wasn't really making enough to support his habit as he wanted to and decided to begin pushing. As a pusher he wasn't much of a success. Everybody soon got wise he wouldn't let you go sick and per result much more was going out than coming in. Eventually one of the cats he'd befriended got caught shooting up and when asked where he scored turned in Elsie's name. I will never forget the shock and the terror of the moment the door was thrust open and a big red-faced cop kind of shouting—"Police"—shoved into the room followed by two more—one who sort of gasped upon seeing Elsie and then turned to one of the others saying—"Get a load of this—degenerate bastard—we sure hit the jackpot this time. This is a queer sonofabitch if I ever saw one. What the hell are these"—as he became aware of the dogs who had gathered around Elsie and were barking and yipping—"God-damned lap dogs—What do they lap on you"—he said as he sort of thrust himself toward Elsie.

Elsie had drawn himself up to his full height and then suddenly began saying—"I'm a hermaphrodite and I've papers to prove it"—and he tried to shove a couple of pamphlets which he used in his sideshow gimmick toward the cop. Meanwhile one of the others had already found our works and the stash of junk—about half an ounce—and was busy tearing Elsie's trunk apart, pulling out the drawers and dumping their contents in the center of the bed. It was when one of the cops stepped on a dog that Elsie began crying.

They took us all down to the city jail on South State Street and since Johnie and I were minors they let us go the next morning.

The last time I saw Elsie was in the Bullpen—sort of cowering in the corner surrounded by a group of young Westside hoods who had been picked up the same night we were—who were exposing themselves to him and yelling all sorts of obscenities.

SPENCER'S PAD

Spencer had a pad on 47th Street. It was one of the coziest pads in New York and one which it was an experience to visit for the first time and to always relax in. It existed in a period when the world was particularly chaotic and New York exceptionally so. For me it represented the one spot at the time where I could seek surcease from tension and invariably find a sense of peace.

Spencer had gone to some pains to make it attractive. He painted the walls a Persian blue and the woodwork a bone white. He kept the lighting soft and had placed big comfortable chairs around his main room. Along one wall he placed his Capehart with records stacked to one side. Long soft Rose drapes hung across his windows. A chest sat between the two windows and oposite a fireplace was a studio couch (the same shade as the drapes) faced with a long coffee table.

Spencer presided over all this with great benevolence and good will, making each of his guests welcome and concerning himself with their wants.

Spencer never used drugs—although I have seen him try pot and recently he told me he had sniffed heroin. But anyone was quite free to use whatever he chose and Spencer always managed to maintain environmental condition conducive to the fullest realization of whatever one happened to be using.

The Capehart was exceptionally fine and acted as a sort of focal point in the pad. Great sounds issued forth from its speaker and filled the whole place with awe inspiring visions. I can recall one incident clearly when the people on 47th Street stood along the curb listening and some were dancing and they were laughing and we were in the window watching while music flowed out on all sides.

At the time the streets of New York teemed with soldiers and sailors—lonely and bewildered—and many found their way to the pad—where for a little while at least life took on some meaning. Often they gave love and always found it. Some discovered God and hardly knew of their discovery. There many heard the great Bird and felt sadness as Lady Day cried out her anguished heart.

Others came also—42nd Street hustlers—poets—simple dreamers, thieves, prostitutes, (both male and female) and pimps and wise guys and junkies and pot heads and just people—seeking sanctuary in a Blue Glade away from the merciless neon glare.

There were young boys who came and swaggered and talked wise and then spoke of their dreams and plans and went away refreshed and aware of themselves as having an identity.

Spencer accepted them all and gave of himself freely to each. The pad was his home and in it he could accept any confession, any seemingly strange behavior, idea, thought, belief and mannerism as part of one, without outward show of censure. Within the confines of his home one could be oneself.

Spencer lost his pad partly because the people in the building in which it was located resented his show of freedom and partly through a situation which developed out of a relationship with a young man.

Vernon was a young man who came to New York in search of a meaning to life. He wanted to write, he wanted to act, he wanted to be loved, he wanted to love, he wanted anything and everything. His background was somewhat more interesting because of having been raised by a father who was a minister of the Baptist church in his home town but who apparently was too busy preaching the gospel to give his own son other than scant attention. His mother had made an effort to make up the difference but her main interest remained with her husband.

Vernon had been in the war and had accomplished nothing except the nickname Angel among his friends because he was always talking about God and because he would listen to anyone's problems. Also he learned to smoke pot.

His appearance was rather striking and upon reaching New York he had no trouble making contacts. Just how he
eventually met Spencer I don't know but meet they did and

became good friends.

One night they had both been out drinking—Vernon smoking pot and both taking nembutals—and had returned to the pad to get some sleep. Both stripped naked and fell on to the bed and into a deep sleep. When they awakened they were in Bellevue.

It seems one or the other must have accidentally brushed against the gas plate opening a valve and that the neighbors, smelling gas in the hallway, upon investigating traced it to Spencer's and being unable to arouse anyone called the police who broke in and finding them both out cold had them rushed to Bellevue, where after reviving them decided they be held for observation. Spencer has since told me, it was a harrowing experience.

Meanwhile the people in the building all got together and signed a petition requesting that Spencer be evicted. As one old queen—who had the apartment next to Spencer's —told me—"My dear—it was really too much. It was a regular black and tan fantasy. Both stark naked—and who knows what they had been doing—Spencer so dark and Vernon pale white. It would have been bad enough if both were the same color. Really, if Spencer wants to end it all he shouldn't try and take one of his lovers with him."

I saw Spencer not long ago and once again he has a charming little place of his own but it isn't quite the 47th Street pad.

RUSSIAN BLACKIE

First time I saw Russian Blackie I was standing at the old Times Square Bar – 42nd Street and 8th Avenue – now long gone—and he was rather weaving back and forth—both arms spread wide—clutching the edge of the bar with his hands—moving his head slowly from side to side—glaring straight ahead toward the huge mirror which made up the back bar—obviously very drunk and as I learned later loaded to his ears on seconal and pot—at this point—tossing off double hookers of straight whiskey. Although the place was crowded with many of the regular habitués—most of whom knew Blackie—immediately around him was a cleared space—no one wishing to get too close to him as he was even when cold sober unpredictable—and drunk—if nothing else—always full of anger and hostility.

Blackie stood about six feet tall and was broad shouldered—neither slim nor heavy. His hair was almost blue black and he never allowed it to become long or unkempt. His facial features were regular and well shaped. He was considered a very handsome man. His eyes were deep brown and when one spoke with him—looking directly into his face it was always difficult to read his expression and one could never be sure whether he was angry or pleased—amused or disgusted—bored or entertained. He was immaculate about his dress—favoring dark colored suits—well tailored and properly fitted—with white shirts and neat conservative ties. In winter his overcoat invariably was of chesterfield styling and frequently he would go without a hat—but always wore gloves and they fitted his hands like another skin.

This was the middle of a cold spell—the wind sharp and penetrating—cutting deep into the marrow of one's bones. Although Blackie was very intoxicated he had somehow retained his dapper appearance. I didn't know anyone I wished to spend time with and didn't remain long at the 44 bar – what time I did stay was spent in observing Blackie and in a sense scrutinizing him. At some point—he found something amusing—and a great smile broke across his countenance. His teeth were large and even and very white and seeing him smile—he stood revealed as a very intriguing and attractive person and the thought flashed through me —he would undoubtedly be a great guy to know.

I departed—and it was several days before I saw Blackie again and this time I was introduced to him. We each acknowledged the introduction and went our respective ways. From then on we would meet every day. Most of these times—we'd say—"Hi"—and keep going—once or twice we had coffee and killed about fifteen or twenty minutes talking about 42nd Street—making scores—the whole Times Square scene—and the usual everyday topics such as weather —the approach of spring and how drunk we'd been the night before. Once in a while I'd see him with other 42nd Street characters. He knew everyone on the Street but when not alone—was usually with a couple of fellows—and knew to be hard core 42nd Street hustlers—who were sharp dressers and reputed to go out occasionally on jobs—maybe a stickup or burglary. I had seen one of them knock a guy flat in one well aimed blow. This same cat later became a good friend of mine—now married and a father—living in Brooklyn. The Russian and I finally became close friends through a series of events which were in a degree cumulative and seemingly unrelated. As I grew more familiar with the environment of Times Square and particularly 42nd Street I learned to at least recognize my neighbors—or the people who lived and participated in the activities of the area. I joined or became part of the crowd that hung around the cafeterias — Bickfords — Chases — Hectors — The Automat and many of the places of business and amusement which remained open all night. I got to know the hotels and stayed in them — sometimes alone but more often with people I'd meet — mostly men and occasionally women. Now and then sitting at the tables with other cats — like myself living principally by their wits — I'd speak of my scores and gradually I became known and trusted — I suppose is the term — best applied when people speak of their exploits in the underworld and expose their secrets. I became acquainted with the thieves who had become professional in their lines — pickpockets — boosters — muggers — a few stick-up men — burglars — and automobile hustlers — and many who never revealed their specialties exactly but hinted at knowing everything in the book — as they might have said.

Talking at different times with various people — frequently we'd be joined by the Russian. Once — he fell in and spoke to me directly about doing him a favor — copping some seconals for him. He had run out it seemed and wouldn't be able to see his druggist until the next day. I had lost no time in locating a drugstore — following my arrival in the city — that supplied me with bennies first — which had just become illegal without prescription. Later the same store sold me anything except narcotics.

I obliged Blackie and copped for him. Next — when he asked me to do the same — I took him with me and introduced him to the druggist. And then one night zonked out of my mind on schmeck — pot — benzedrine and seconals I met a cat I had become friendly with who was a kind of John or mark. He would come to 42nd Street after finishing work at his place of employment. He was lonely and attracted to young men of the knock around — Times Square hipster — hustler types. He was a good spender and one always ate — and could get a flop and beside he came on fairly straight and one could relax and pretty much be themselves with him. We spoke for a few minutes and he commented about how high I appeared and added that although he expected to see a friend from around the Squrae he'd promised to give money to and if I understood I couldn't expect to receive any money in the morning — he would like to meet the cat and come along.

I accepted the invitation and met Blackie for the first time in an environment away from the hard core 42nd Street. He proved to be an amazingly congenial and affable companion — obviously well versed in ways of being entertaining and agreeable. Apparently he had known our host many years and from parts of the conversation between them I gathered — although their acquaintance began in the usual fashion for both of them — it soon ripened into a friendship of mutual respect. Blackie seemingly delighted in telling of his exploits and one could sense the amusement he stressed conversationally as being part of his interest in all of his activities involving the manner in which he lived and at one point — he told of taking advantage of several opportunities to make money — and named several people they both knew — as victims — while they both gossiped and reminisced. Both were conscientious about keeping me posted — frequently drawing me into communication — asking if I was aware of a particular place — or building — or had I seen a particular person hanging around Bickford's — giving quick biographical and descriptive clues as to exactly who they might be discussing.

We all three got very high on seconals and ale.

At any rate — from then on — Blackie — became part of my life with a certain consistency and we remained in close proximity — our relationship with various people overlapped and we shared experiences together.

We were never as close as Blackie was with many people but a sort of bond grew and existed between us. There are innumerable aspects of his personality I wasn't aware of and would be pressed to analyze. We did share a kind of love and mutual regard for each other.

There was a reserve and hardness in him difficult to penetrate — yet there was always a straightness — perhaps — or consciousness of beauty in all of his actions.

The Russian — as he was frequently called among his more intimate associates — impressed me and my life became — in a sense — richer or greater for having known him.

I suppose there were women in his life during the time I knew him — important and emotionally involved with him — but oddly it was his closest friend's girl and later wife — Blackie showed interest in — and spent much time with. His friend Frank trusted him implicitly — nor do I think his trust was ever misused — (Blackie had the old fashioned concept of loyalty — believing — one does not covet his neighbor's wife.) I am inclined to think perhaps — she may have tried resting her womanly charms but the Russian stood firm. They all three remained staunch friends and after the marriage and the arrival of the first child it was amusing to see Blackie — red eyed and angry — appearing — glaring — defiantly out toward the shadowed corners of the room — ready to sweep clean the darkness of lurking danger in defense of 47

Frank Junior — proud and pleased with the responsibility of baby sitting.

There was a slight change in Blackie's personality and general requirements after Frank married. Where once there had been a partner to rely on — at a moment's notice — it became a matter of operating alone — more often than not. He was and may still be an effective hustler. Still he did become more settled and was less apt to be seen staggering from one side to the other — ready for a slug fest or to simply belt someone for the hell of it. Two years after the birth of the first baby there was a second baby and by this time Blackie was well trained.

We ran into each other about a year ago. Except for a little more weight and less ebulience — he is very much as he has always been.

DETROIT REDHEAD — 1943-1947

When I first met her she was about eighteen. I was sitting in the 42nd Street Bickford restaurant drinking coffee and talking with a character known as Johnie Pimples — a young cat — a typical 42nd Street hustler — open for any suggestion where a dollar was involved but mostly at the time making it with fags for a place to sleep — a couple of bucks eating and show money occasionally scoring a ten spot or a twenty — spending it on clothes — a chick — across the bar on his acquaintances — while he gave them a rundown on how smart he had been beating the queer — or how some day he was going to go to Los Angeles — maybe try and get in the movies — if he could only get rid of all these goddamned pimples. He had heard a lot of actors had had bad skin but that what with the latest developments in plastic surgery there wasn't anything they couldn't do — that is if a guy was photogenic — which incidentally didn't always mean a guy had to be especially good-looking. He knew he was photogenic because some gay photographer — one who always came looking just for him — wouldn't pick up anybody else — good for a sawbuck every time — had told him so.

We had been talking about Pimples' brother — who was some kind of big shot — in Brooklyn — something to do with the rackets — who didn't like Johnie — wouldn't let him in the house when he went home. His brother was boss since his mother had died. His old man stayed drunk most of the time and since his brother paid the bills there wasn't anything he could do. We were both sitting facing the street — Pimples had just finished telling me how some day he was going to have a place of his own — make a lot of money — and he'd bet sometime his brother would need a few bucks and that it would sure give him a lot of pleasure to tell him to go to hell — when I watched her walk by — slowly — head held high — carefully looking everyone over — half smiling as she noticed Pimples and continuing on down the street. She was wearing a simple plain skirt of some dark 49 material — a soft pink sweater — loose and fluffy — a single strand of pearl beads around her throat — hardly any makeup and later I discovered — she had on a pair of saddle type oxfords. At first glance she looked about sixteen and not at all typical of the usual chick found walking alone on 42nd Street glancing in Bickford's window.

I commented to Pimples about her and he said he knew her. He said she had just busted with Knuckles. Knuckles was one of the local pimps and was known for the rough way he handled his girls — also because most of his girls were fine. According to Pimples this one had hit town somewhere from the Middle West. Knuckles had spotted her coming out of the 50th Street bus terminal — somehow began a conversation with her — taken her to his pad — kept her there under lock and key until she finally began co-operating. He had broken her in with several of the 42nd Street hustlers — just to get her started and recently she had cut out with some trick who had eyes for her — didn't care she was a whore — and had set her up on her own — threatening Knuckles with the cops or something like that if he didn't leave her alone.

We continued to sit and talk when shortly she came back and walked into the place and up to our table. She glanced at me and then spoke to Pimples asking him if he had seen someone called Larry. Pimples said he hadn't and asked her to join us for coffee. Pimples got up and walked over to the counter to get her coffee and she sat down at the table and asked me for a cigarette. We talked and she spoke of having come from Detroit and one or two experiences she had encountered. Then she began talking about Knuckles and how green she had been but that now she was beginning to learn her way around and there would never be another episode like that one for her to contend with. She opened her purse and took out a pair of brass knucks which she explained she always carried with her and "I've got this also" — she said as she removed a switch-blade knife from her bag snapping the blade open. "I can use it — if necessary — although I hope it is never necessary — I hate violence." Meanwhile Pimples had returned with coffee for all of us. We sat drinking the coffee and when we had finished we decided to leave — Pimples had a meet with a fag who — so he said — was good for a double sawbuck — and Vickie suggested if I had nothing better to do I walk her as far as the subway at Seventh Avenue. There was something attractive and enthusiastic — warm and beautiful about her.

I was living on the Lower East Side — Henry Street — with an old ex-show queen named Bozo — and a fellow I had met on 42nd Street and had hung around with all that past winter and spring — André — very much the ladies' man — whose real name was Fred Veda. He had lived most of his life in Yonkers, New York. He had left home and was hanging around 42nd Street — picking up a few bucks here and there — mostly from the colored homosexuals that go down to 42nd Street and look for lovers and young men. He was well liked by them and had known some for many years. He had lived at one time in the Village with a colored poet. He had met Bozo and Bozo loved him and invited him to share his apartment. André had accepted Bozo and while I had run into some difficulty in a place I had been living he and Bozo invited me to stay with them.

While walking with Vickie I suggested perhaps she might like meeting a friend of mine and to come on down to my place for a while. She said she had other plans for the evening but she would like to fall in some other time. We made arrangements for seeing each other again. We became friends.

Vickie wasn't a beautiful girl in the generally accepted sense of the word. She was self-conscious of her height and when we first met she had been in the habit of carrying herself slightly round shouldered to minimize her tallness. Her hair was an almost mahogany red she wore shoulder length — softly waved and lightly fluffed at the ends. Her skin was pale with a dusting of freckles. Her eyes green and rather widely spaced were expressive and always held a sort of bewildered gentle look of innocence. Her mouth was a bit wide with a full underlip and very red. Her body was beautiful with long legs and small well shaped breasts firm and high she never encased in a brassière. Her movements were graceful and when she walked she took long free steps. She wasn't beautiful but decidedly striking in appearance and later when she became a bit more confident 51 of herself and took to wearing more glamorous type clothes she was something to see cutting down the street.

She was a strange mixture of gentleness and extreme violence. She was filled with doubts and confusion. She was lonely and rushed about seeking love and understanding. She felt very much alone. She was unable to make any sort of adjustment — would try and conform only to find herself unhappy feeling rejected. There was a certain strain of creativeness within her she was unable to release causing her frustration. She was a dreamer — a lover of the sun and the river. She liked to walk and many the night we walked all night long ending up in Chinatown for breakfast.

She became well known and had many people interested in her. Most of the cats from the Times Square area knew her and were in love with her to some extent. There were several chicks she made it with.

Her mother had died when she was a young child and she had been raised by her father. She had a great love for her father and it was when she discovered he was homosexual she had left home. Eventually she became more understanding and learned to accept his deviation — this after she had experienced love for the first time.

Vickie was living up in the 70's in an old brown stone front. She had a large first floor room with two huge windows that reached from the ceiling to the floor. One could step from either window to stone balustrades on the sides of the steps to the sidewalk. The room was oblong in shape with high ceilings. One entered thru two large sliding doors. Opposite the doors was a big mirror built into the wall. Vickie arranged a small lamp with a dim bulb immediately in front using it as the only light. A street lamp burning outside cast light in thru the windows.

She met André and they fell in love. She had kept her appointment with me and I took her down to my place and they met. He was good looking and should have lived during the time of buccaneers — flowing capes and hats with plumes. He knew New York from one end to the other and soon he and Vickie were to be seen at any hour in almost any part of the city. They went for long walks and spent hours talking and dreaming of what the future might hold for them. They loved each other unstintingly and planned to get married until his family stepped into the scene and let him know in no uncertain terms they wouldn't tolerate his marrying a whore. Vickie had tricked with his father at a convention and was embarrassed and ashamed when André invited her home to meet his people and they were introduced. It upset her far more than it did André, but his father nearly hit the ceiling when he learned they were planning marriage. The plans for the marriage fell thru.

Vickie continued living an active life — meeting people — settling down to a more practical attitude concerning her prostitution — lining up several johns who were regular weekly customers contributing various sums of money — from one who paid her fifty dollars to one who was giving her one hundred fifty — moving from a one room apartment to a three room apartment — buying furniture — new clothes — occasionally acting as a fence — buying and selling stolen articles of jewelry — learning to play drums — making it with the Bop musicians — being seen at Birdland. The Royal Roost — swinging up to Harlem — eventually picking up steady with a cat who was a junky — beginning to take an occasional joy-pop herself. Every now and then I would run into her and we would sit and talk — usually over coffee — in some cafeteria but I wasn't seeing her steady during that time. She said she had gotten pretty hung up on André and it was a disappointment things hadn't worked out per plan. She said she guessed that was life and that now since she had organized her life — such as it was — perhaps it was as well she hadn't married. She was still seeing André off and on and they would spend a day or two together — but the big passion had cooled down. Once I ran into her one morning about five A.M. in Kelloggs Cafeteria on 49th Street — a hang out for a big group of Times Square pimps — whores — thieves — show people — musicians — pot heads — and junkies. She was with two brothers just in from Cleveland, Ohio. I don't know exactly how they had met originally but she apparently had known them for some time and they sat reminiscing about some of their past experiences. She introduced them as Bob and Don Brandenburgh and at the same time told me — "They are the greatest. Get to know them." Later — after I did get to know them — Bob told me he had met Vickie about a month prior to when we met and 53

that they had been introduced by one of the musicians —
blowing sax up at the Roost – he had known in Cleveland.
He had looked him up when he hit town – looking to cop
some pot. He and the cat had fallen up to Vickie's and she
had turned them on. He and Vickie had eyes for each other
so he had made it with her until having to return to Cleveland.
He had gone back to Cleveland — taken care of some bus-
iness — picked up his brother Don — and it was just after
they had returned to New York we met.

Don was a merchant seaman and had come to New
York to get a ship.

Vickie suggested — since she had a meet with one of
her johns later in the morning — I take Bob and Don down-
town with me. She said they were nearly broke and were
tired. She sipped me a couple of sticks of pot and told me to
light up when we got home.

Bozo and André had been in the process of severing
their friendship for the past few weeks — and Bozo took an
immediate liking to Bob. He suggested Bob and Don stay
with us until they could make other arrangements. André
took an instant dislike to both Bob and Don and decided to
move out immediately. We all managed to settle in comfor-
tably. Don and I spent most of our time looking for a ship. I
had decided to go back to sea and we both thought we
would enjoy making a trip together. We finally got what we
were looking for in the way of a ship — and made abut an
eight month trip. It was one of the best trips I made while
going to sea.

When we returned Don decided to go back to Cleveland.
Meanwhile Bozo and André split up and Bob and I took
over Bozo's apartment and turned it into a tea pad and
thieves' den. There were four or five fellows making the
place a sort of headquarters. They would spend the night
going out and scoring — coming in — in the mornings — with
quarts of beer — pot — bennies and a friend or a chick and
we would sit around and ball — people sometimes falling
asleep — so there was some kind of action constantly.

We painted the walls black with yellow panels and a
Chinese red ceiling. Long black and yellow drapes hung to
the floor over the windows. A crescent shaped lamp with a
54 red bulb hung from a cord — suspended over a black L

shaped couch. There was a distinct oriental opium-den atmosphere.

Meanwhile Vickie had gotten hooked on junk. When I got in touch with her – she invited me to come up to her room. She had lost her three room apartment and all her furniture and was living in one room up on 102nd Street just off Central Park West in a strange building – with all sorts of unnecessary staircases – hallways – different levels on each floor – little closets and cupboards in the hallways all painted different colors so the whole effect was almost surrealistic – and most of the people living there – even strange. There were musicians of all kinds – bop – jazz – hillbilly – pop singers – even one old man who used to sit out in front on the stoop – twanging a Jew's harp. There were various types of show people – including a group of out-of-work midgets – who quarreled and screamed at each other all hours of the day and night. There were several young college students from Columbia – three old ladies who were always drunk and sat in a room on the first floor near the entrance every day with the door open – a half gallon of wine on the table – watching everybody who came in and out – or what a bitch she is – or he beats his wife – etc., loud enough so people could hear. And then there was Vickie and her group of friends most of whom were using junk.

I began seeing Vickie regularly and using junk with her. In fact – although I didn't give up my interest in the pad downtown completely – I moved in with her.

She had changed considerably from the young innocent girl I had first known. There was still the quality of gentleness and wide-eyed wonder about her but on the surface there was a patina of indifference. Somewhere along the line that certain spark of aliveness distinguishing her from the other girls – that special little flame so completely hers – had been quenched. She now lived entirely in a world of fantasy. We spent hours – simply sitting – listening to music. She had managed to keep her phonograph and records – and would place a stack on the changer – then lie back – listening.

Somehow we managed to get by financially even though our habits were costing – twenty five to thirty five dollars a day. She had kept two of her johns and would see them 55 every week. I still had some money from my trip and was doing some stealing. We lived together – in this way for about five months – all through the summer and up until almost Christmas of that year. We had a rather beautiful kind of love – devoid of tension – anxiety – and emotional violence. We were at peace with each other and I look back to that time with a deep feeling of gratitude.

Just about Christmas things began going bad for both of us. We were having trouble keeping our habits going. Money was becoming difficult to obtain and we had gone sick once or twice – making us irritable. We had an argument where we both said miserable things to each other. Things got so bad we couldn't make the rent and Vickie was afraid to go out and leave her things because the landlord might lock the door. Finally we decided to pack everything up and move downtown.

Most of the cats making the scene downtown kind of fell in love with her. She babied them – listened to their troubles – let them tell her about their dreams and plans – played music for them – read them poetry – so they understood it – for the first time. Occasionally – when one or two of them had a job they intended pulling – breaking into and entering a store – they would take her along – and then when they got back – would talk about how cool she had been or how much heart she had.

The bathtub was in the kitchen and it was entertaining to watch Vickie bathe. She was beautiful sitting in the tub – her hair piled up on the top of her head – the tub overflowing with frothy bubble bath – heavily scented with something called Shanghai.

One morning she had one fellow painting his toenails silver. He was just out of prison – having served almost ten years. He never forgot Vickie and years later when I ran into him he asked about her – he said – "Man that was some redhead."

She used to go out alone and cut around the city and she took to wearing our clothes. She would put on a suit and a man's shirt or sometimes she would go glamorous in a dress and high heels.

About this time a young Italian cat named Ricci began hanging around the pad. He became friendly with Bob and they formed a partnership. They planned a caper in Washington D.C. and spent much time rushing back and forth between the two cities. Finally they made the take in Washington – but at the last minute – when they were making their getaway – one of them dropped a matchpad with a telephone number on it. The cops found it – traced the number and grabbed them in Washington. We got the news about 3:30 in the morning. One of Ricci's boys from Long Island came by and told us – we had better clear out before the police had a chance to locate the pad.

Vickie and I packed up – bag and baggage – called a second hand furniture man – sold everything in the place to him and were out and gone by two o'clock the following afternoon.

Vickie had met a young cat who lived in Philly and had pleaded with her to make the scene in Philly with him. She decided to take him up on it – figuring it was a good idea to get out of New York at the time. We said good-bye and it was nearly two years until I saw her again.

Things continued to go along pretty rough for me until I took a fall for possession of a five dollar bag of heroin and was sentenced to six months on Rikers Island. I served the six months – actually less than six – since I got five days a month off for good behavior. When I came out – I had of course kicked my habit – cold turkey – while in prison – I was very careful – not doing any stealing – getting by bumming off friends and acquaintances until I got a job on a ship and went back to sea. The following winter – shortly after coming back – I went down to Texas and stayed not quite a year with a friend. After returning to New York in the late Fall – I again got hung up on drugs – acquired a partner who taught me how to burglarize. I worked with him – until the middle of the summer – when we split up – because he wanted to go back to his home town. My habit was pretty heavy by this time and again I found the going rough. I was just barely getting by – I was spending everything I'd get my hands on for junk and didn't even have a place to live. When I had about reached the end of my endurance – I was sick half the time – run down physically – without a place to sleep – dirty – worn out – my feet sore and bleeding – ready for suicide – a friend I hadn't seen for 57 some time – and ran into on the street – took pity on me. He let me sleep in his place. It was days – many days – before I could get up and get around. I was exhausted and slept – twenty and twenty-four hours at a stretch. I was more dead than alive and wanted it that way. I didn't want to live. Prayed for death.

Eventually I began coming out of it – although emotionally and mentally I was defeated. I began going out on the streets again – and one night at the corner of 50th and Broadway I ran into Vickie. She was looking extremely well – dressed in a black silk coat and gold wool dress. When she saw me – she held her coat in both hands spreading it out like wings – and sort of running toward me she reminded me of a big black and gold butterfly. She told me she had been doing quite well – until but recently working as a model – doing a little hustling on the side – living up near Columbia – over close to the river and was half in love with Ricci who she had been seeing quite a lot of since returning to New York. She said she had done fairly well in Philly but had gotten homesick for New York. She was vague about what had happened in Philly except to say that she had spent only a short time with the man she had gone there to see. She mentioned having had various jobs – none of which suited her very long. She had kept in touch with Bob and Ricci – having contacted Don in Cleveland and although Bob was still serving time – Ricci had been home about six months. He had driven down to Philly with a friend about a month ago and they had balled for about a week. He asked her to come on up to New York and here she was. She also told me – she was using stuff again – in fact both she and Ricci were – so she explained – half hooked. She had kicked her habit in Philly but when Ricci came on the scene he had some stuff with him and she had picked up. She said she was just on her way to cop and suggested I go along. She said Ricci was waiting for her to come back to her place and after she made her meet we would go up there and get straight.

I joined her and from then on we began seeing each other consistently. Ricci was doing fine but spent much of his time out on the Island with his people. Vickie would stop by where I was living and sometimes we would sit and talk or go out and see a movie. Occasionally Ricci would come along with his car and we would take long drives.

Ricci was anxious to make a big score and he had cased several places out on the Island he thought might be good takes. One afternoon – we made one of the spots and although the take wasn't big it did get us straight financially for a while. From then on we operated regularly. Things were getting better when one early evening the three of us got caught. Ricci had said – "This is a sure thing" – and per result we were overly confident and that was it. We were taken to the Long Island City prison. Ricci and myself were held there for trial and Vickie was taken to the Women's House of Detention in New York City.

I saw very little of Vickie after that. I learned that she had finally broken down and written her father who immediately flew to New York, bailed her out of prison, obtaining permission to take her back to Detroit until the day of the trial. I saw her in the court room on the day of the trial and again on the day of sentencing. On the day of sentencing she stood beside me, looking pale and tired. She was wearing something plain. Her hair was neatly combed and she stood with her head bowed. She glanced at me once, and for a moment her eyes lit up and a tiny smile touched her mouth, then once again she looked down and there was little of the Vickie I had first seen and known. The judge gave her a five year suspended sentence and they whisked her out of the courtroom. That was the last time I saw her.

I went upstate to prison for five years and Ricci was sent to Pilgrim State Hospital.

Almost a month ago I ran into a girl Vickie and I had known and she told me she had made a trip to Detroit last year and had looked Vickie up. She said Vickie had married and has two children. She said she is very much the typical suburban matron and is active in the P.T.A. We both laughed and agreed we could see her organizing the good mothers of the P.T.A. and that Vickie was surely the one to do it.

I probably knew Vickie better than most of the people she was acquainted with here in New York, and I wonder what she has done about all her dreams and how she has managed to curb her enthusiasm for excitement and adventure. Basically she was one of the most honest women I 59 have ever known.

There are few spots in the city I can go without being reminded that Vickie was there once also.

TATTOOED WOMAN

I had walked part way up the block on 29th Street between 8th and 9th Avenue – thinking how strange – unlike New York this whole scene. The feeling of space was what made the difference. The entire area below 29th Street, as far down as perhaps 27th Street from 8th Avenue to 10th or 11th Avenue, is wide open where buildings have been torn down leaving only rubble. It is as though a great iron claw had reached down from the sky squeezing picking laying flat everything standing above ground scooping it up letting it drop between the pinchers back to the earth to lie forgotten. In the distance toward the river a tall needle thin steeple silhouetted against the color wracked sky of sunset, the sun a disk of angry red. Destruction and decay. The houses facing the scene set back from the street-yards rampant with tall weeds, grass-green stuff crawling up the sides with tiny purple and red flowers. Windows broken, rotting wooden banisters and steps with people sitting listless and tired. Half naked children playing in the grass. A child on a tricycle, naked to the waist, a pair of dirty blue jeans – exposing half his buttocks, a toy pistol holstered banging against his hip, scooted along side me as I returned toward neon flushed 8th Avenue. A young hip looking Puerto Rican standing alongside the lamppost called to the boy as we reached the corner: "Hey – cowboy." The boy laughed racing off down the street shouting: "bang-bang-bang."

Eighth Avenue had already taken on evening activities. Several young chicks came bouncing by, the hipster watching them. Three or four men came out of the bar talking. A few people shuffling along, heads hanging, looking at the sidewalk, oblivious of their surroundings. Sound of jukebox, traffic, usual city noises, rumble of the subway below the street.

The sky had paled into twilight. The reds and greens of the stop lights standing out more distinctly. Headlights of the automobiles.

I was hungry, deciding to stop in the Riker's for something to eat before returning home. Entering, I was instantaneously aware of a woman standing in front of a large wall mirror looking at herself adjusting the skirt of her dress. On her upper arm near the shoulder – a tattoo – "Toni." I passed by her glancing casually in her direction – observing in a flash her striking appearance. She was tall with gray streaked black hair hanging in large loose waves immediately below her shoulders, brushed back behind one ear, one lock fixed flat against her cheek in a spit curl. In her ear an ornate coral and white earring – like flower petals. Her complexion was almost swarthy. She was heavily made up, large mouth painted a vivid scarlet. Her clothing was nondescript almost shabby. Her dress black, sleeveless, bound in around the waist by a wide black patent leather belt. She wore extremely high heels and carried a black purse.

Her presence dominated the room. As I sat down at the counter I noticed her speaking with a man who had come in after me. I couldn't hear the conversation but suddenly she raised her voice telling him to go to hell. She began sauntering toward the counter swinging her purse with an air of unconcern. Reaching the counter she walked along until sitting next to me. As she seated herself, she said to me: "I hate a phony. Baby I wouldn't attend a dog fight with that prick." She called to the counter man – "Hey sweetheart – coffee – heavy with the cream." Meanwhile she placed her purse on the counter leaning it against the sugar container. She then arranged her skirt – afterward patting her hair.

Upon close inspection I realized her age must be well into the thirties, perhaps forty. There were deep lines going downward from the sides of her nose almost reaching the jaw. Beneath her eyes dark heavily shadowed pockets. Her mouth corners drawn downward as though showing contempt for all she was surrounded by. On one of her hands another tattoo—the sign of the Pachuca. Her arms showed scars from wrist to shoulder. Old needle marks – tracks – where she had tried to hit her veins and missed. Her eyes were glazed, constantly closing, the pupils pin points. A junky. Her hands were puffy and dirty, the fingernails painted loud pink, the polish chipped, several nails broken. Occasionally she would look down the counter to where the man she had spoken with was sitting, mumbling – "the bastard, the phony bastard" – then looked straight ahead, slightly nodding.

PONDEROSA PINE

You speak of Ponderosa Pine and I am catapulted back – oh way back and it is late summer outside Potlatch, Idaho. It is sunset – the sky riven with saffron – ice green – lavender and changing pinks from flamingo to palest hue overlaid with haunting black cloud shapes. The road is yellow dirt and sand packed down and spread with rough cut white stone and gravel. It twists through the cluster of grey clapboard houses – past a railroad track – a train of flat cars loaded with massive tree trunks fresh cut from the vast forests covering the hills for miles and miles around – too huge for the saw mill – a painted red wood frame building on the edge of the community – where many of the town's people work – the others employed mostly in the forests – axing – cutting – felling – hauling the great majestic trees – the countryside reverberating all day with the agonizing thuds of their crashing death – and we are in an open Model T Ford and we pass the saw mill – the general store – a beer parlor – where on several occasions just before this time I am speaking of – I have gotten drunk downing the frothing pitchers of ice cold beer brought to the table by a dark haired bar maid – wise in the ways of a beer parlor in a lumber town able to laugh and toss joke for joke with the red faced heavy bodied lumberjacks – still wearing their caulked boots – I once saw two of them in a fight – and when one had fallen – the other stomped on his face in fury until the face looked like a hunk of raw beef when he was finally rescued – and red and black – green and black – orange and black – blue and black checked shirts and all this in a flash in my mind as the road rounds the last of the houses – the evening darkening blue-black in the distance bedizened with the lights of thousands upon thousands of cosmic worlds the stars and planets. The road now heads into the forests – only the tops of the great trees still visible individually – seemingly brushing the sky – all below a great mass of blackness the headlights penetrating the mass – revealing brown tree trunks on either side and green foliage – the limbs of the trees begin too high up for us to see them. My companion is a young Norwegian boy – seventeen – the son of one of the foresters at the ranger station near Potlatch. It is his father's job along with two or three others to keep up on the maintenance of the firetowers – to patrol the area and keep weather reports. The father has made this his life work and is a good but stern man who has raised his son – he hopes – to follow in his footsteps. The son is extremely proud of his father and will in all probability do as his father desires. When he returns from this little excursion or trip he has invited me to accompany him on – I had wandered up into that part of the country several weeks prior and had asked if they had some work I could do around the ranger station and they said yes – and I stayed until leaving on this trip which was to take us over into Montana to visit relatives – a cousin or uncle – if I remember correctly – of my traveling companion – he will be ready to enter agriculture college at Moscow, Idaho. He is not very talkative and I sit back drinking in the heady aroma of the pine forest almost intoxicated by the richness of the beauty of the night.

We drive steadily thru the night – stopping once in a small town at a lunch room for great steaming mugs of coffee and thick sandwiches of ham and cheese and home-made blackberry pie – then on – spelling each other at the wheel – the road always winding and twisting – alongside rushing streams for several miles up into the hills – past ravines and valleys – once up the side of a mountain – the road zig-zagging all the way up and then all the way down the opposite side. Once in a while we hit stretches of pavement but for the most part the road remained dirt and gravel.

Dawn found us not far from the town of Kellogg, Idaho – a good sized town where we stopped and freshened up in cold spring water – checked the condition of our car – drank coffee – discussed our further route. It was decided we drive thru the Coeur d'Alene country and around the Coeur d'Alene Lake after which we would pick a highway leading up over and thru mountain ranges into Montana.

The topography had changed and we now hit stretches 65

of flat open country with mountains way off in the distance. Huge rocks and boulders lay in all directions. The soil was full of rocks and there were only a few gnarled and twisted live oak trees to be seen instead of the lush green forests. We arrived in Coeur d'Alene – drove thru and picked up a road following the shore of the lake – brilliant blue and clear – the shore line ragged and stony – short windblown and twisted trees leaning toward their reflections in the water. A wind had sprung up and massive cloud formations plowed across the blue sky. The water of the lake became choppy – the surface agitated with small rolling white caps. The scene was magnificent and awe inspiring – beautiful and cold and real. I filled myself with it and can at this instant not only see it all vividly but smell the freshness of air – and hear the whistling of the wind.

We eventually reached the end of this wonderful stretch of earth and water – coming down off the lake road onto a paved highway leading directly into the mountains to be crossed into Montana. We began climbing – higher and higher – until our engine was heated and we were carrying a banner of white stream smoke fro the radiator cap at the front of the car. Half way up we came upon a small place at the side of the road where we pulled in to rest a while. Near was a fresh mountain stream rushing downward where we filled cans and poured them into our hot and thirsty car.

The weather had begun to change and to one side of us and back over the jutting angry looking peaks of the seemingly endless chain of mountains we could see rolling grey and black clouds constantly illuminated by flashes of lightning and accompanied by reverberating rumbles of thunder relentlessly bearing down on us.

Once again we began the ascent – slowly crawling toward the top. We had no means of protection against the storm – there was no top for the car and when it hit there would be nothing to do but let it drive down on us.

Gradually we reached the top and looking back could see the black rain curtain – feel the on-coming rush of rain laden wind. At the top of the mountain was a short distance of straight road bound on either side with fairly dense growth of tall and at this time writhing trees. As we started

to drive this respite of straight terrain – high up above the world – near the lowering furiously rolling clouds the full force of the storm struck and we could go no further. We pulled over a little onto the shoulder of the road and stopped.

The wind a mass of heavy raindrops relentlessly tore at us as though infuriated at not being able to lift us from our spot and fling us crashing into the heavy grey boulders just ahead – abating an instant and then with renewed vigor attacking our flimsy little car – shaking it and rocking it with the fury and force of its anger. Long jagged sulphurous bolts of lightning drove with full force into the earth around us filling our nostrils with the smell of burning ozone. Thunder crashed deafeningly down and around our heads and all the earth trembled. The roadway became a rushing flow of water – a tree was struck – and split in a great screech the top half falling toward the ground pulling the wound open further, the life of the tree no longer protesting. With this sacrifice to the greed of the storm – it began to slacken passing on over – only occasional flashes of lightning and instead of crashing thunder there were only low rumblings becoming fainter in the distance. The rain had ceased altogether – the clouds began clearing away and soon the sun – bright and warming appeared.

We of course were thoroughly drenched and what was worse unable to start the car. We worked with it – checking the motor – cranking – but all to no avail. It was utterly impossible to get it moving. Finally we hailed a passing car and asked for a tow to the first filling station. The people — a man and his wife — were accommodating and towed us down to a station the other side of the mountain in Montana. There we discovered all was lost – not only were things flooded but completely burned out – the Model T had had it – it would carry us no further.

My friend was very disappointed but decided it best to call his father. He called and his father said we were to stay near our present location – the boy's mother would pick us up in the family car the following day.

We stayed in a motel cabin not far from where we had made the call. He was very disappointed with the entire experience and failed to share my enthusiastic impression of the storm – nor was he impressed by what I considered the wild almost breathtaking beauty of the lake and the 67 forests we had driven thru – saying at one point – he supposed they did have beauty but in his opinion they were just a lake and a forest – and a forest was a forest no matter what one said about it – and yes the storm was sort of exciting but he would rather have his Model T working – after all he'd earned the money to pay for it and now it was just a loss.

His mother arrived the next afternoon and we drove straight back to the ranger station near Potlatch.

I guess he had decided I wasn't a very stable kind of person because although I remained several days at the station before leaving to head back home – he never came around to say hello and once or twice his father who had always in our short acquaintance been friendly and considerate – was somewhat sharp in his replies to questions I asked him.

Anyhow – you spoke of Ponderosa Pine – and this was Ponderosa Pine country – and I remember it all clearly. Of course there was Tamarack and yellow pine and white pine – but Ponderosa is a beautiful name – and maybe – just maybe – there really wasn't any Ponderosa there at all – but please let it suffice – of the other three – white and yellow pine and Tamarack I am sure – and somewhere in the past I've been around Ponderosa country of that you may be confident. It is only that I am a little forgetful these days – just where all the things I've been around or near are located.

I wouldn't have bothered with further explanations except – I dislike being caught in an outright lie – and it is just possible Ponderosa Pine is strictly native of California and it would be most embarrassing to hear this – after having given it root – in a manner of speaking – in wild rugged Idaho. And at this point – that is right this moment that will already be of the past – when you hear of it – or read of it – I sincerely believe that by now Ponderosa Pine must thrive in Idaho and that if it wasn't there when I was there – someone planted it there – and in no time it began to flourish.

The forests of Idaho are or at least were truly wild and beautiful. The great tall trees reaching to the sky and on the stillest days – with hardly a breeze stirring near the earth – one hears the whishing of the tree tops way up high enough to always feel the wind. And at their feet – wild flowers –

ferns – flowing streams – berry bushes and morning glory vines. Sometimes of course – they have grown very close together in groves like clusters on the sides of the mountains – and no sun has penetrated down through to the earth – there is only blankets of dark brown needles sere and dry.

There is wild life – deer and bear – pheasant and grouse – rabbit and squirrels – there are only non poisonous snakes – and many kinds of birds.

As I said before it is surely Ponderosa Pine country -and if anyone asks you to visit Idaho – make sure you don't refuse – and if I am around still – please please see if you can swing the invitation for me as well. Every now and then it all comes back to me in a rush and strange as it may sound coming from an old drug soaked city character like myself – I long to see all I have spoken of and much I've left unsaid – again. Perhaps my most carefree hours were spent there – and maybe it is impossible to recapture any of it – but I sure as hell – occasionally long to give it a try.

JOHNNIE I

It was in 1948 – January during a siege of severe New York winter weather. It had snowed for several days – stopped – clearing up – growing milder – the snow melting into dirty slush – then becoming intensely cold – snowing again – covering the streets in white mounds on top of frozen soot mottled piles of banked snow – burying automobiles in white shrouds – wind driven tiny ice pellets. Traffic had come almost to a standstill – crawling through the rushes of whistling wind – huddled in coats – ear muffs – scarves sweaters – gloves – shoulders hunched – from doorway to doorway – to restaurants – subway entrances – seeking shelter along sides of the great graystone buildings. At night the city streets became even more deserted with only a few to be seen on 42nd Street – probably one of the busiest streets of any city in the world – a few like myself living in cafeterias – sleeping in the all night movies – staying away from the cops on their beats – who were angry to be out – glad of any excuse to pick a man up – hurry him to the nearest station house in out of the cold – or – walking through the underground tunnels down toward the Penn Station – through the Station into the restrooms – sitting on the toilets sleeping – sometimes writing – looking to pick someone up who had money and wanted sex – willing to pay for it – anxious only for a place to sleep – take a bath – shave – obtain clean clothing – even food. Maybe steal a suitcase – roll a stray drunk – meet a friend – talk – make it till the morning and a cheap movie. I had been living in this manner since shortly after the beginning of the New Year. I was broke – hungry most of the time – poorly clad for contesting the rage of the elements – staying awake using Benzedrine inhalers – occasionally smoking pot – somehow maintaining a junk habit – just managing to keep straight enough not to collapse completely – stealing – ready to make a dollar at anything – always looking for a good take – something big enough to allow me a chance for a bed of my own – a place to live or at least die in out of the cold – not to be found crouched – a corpse in the doorway. I wanted to die and felt I was dying – could observe death feeding on me – see it in the pallor of my skin – the patches of oozing sores on my chin and face – in the tiny red flecks in the whites of my eyes – in the way my skull showed through the skin at the temples and I could smell it from my dirt coated bleeding feet – from my crotch – from my clothing.

Sometimes I'd be lucky finding Allen home – who would permit me to sleep for fourteen or fifteen hours – then giving me money enough for food and Benzedrine – suggesting I look for a job – trying to give me incentive – sensing my desolation. His was the only love I knew for a long stretch of time – my only contact with life – and I stole from him – hocking the articles for enough money to get a bag of junk.

It was on a Sunday morning and the snow storm had abated. Exceedingly cold winds swept thru the city. A winter sun hung dimly glistening in a smoke gray sky. I had seen Frenchy – a 42nd Street fence – who had a monster-like appearance – large of body with a big round pock-marked face – with small beady piglike eyes – a large nearly hairless head sitting on a big thick neck – several rolls of fat sticking out over the back of his collar – his skin the color and texture of clay – enter Horn & Hardart's Automat on 42nd Street and having stolen a pair of good leather gloves – from a guy sitting next to me as I rested in the Penn Station – I figured I might be able to talk Frenchy out of a couple of dollars. It was about 11 A.M. and the place was fairly crowded. I had coffee money with me – walked directly toward the coffee spigot – glancing at the crowd – obtained the coffee – walking then over to the table occupied by Frenchy becoming aware en route – Frenchy had been joined by two young men about 20 years of age in appearance – both neat – one quite light in complexion – the other darker – dressed in the uniform sharpie style of the period. They were talking loudly – obviously aware of the people around them – boasting about what an easy job it had been – holding a wristwatch by the band strap – just below the level of the table top asking Frenchy to buy it – as I sat down. Frenchy greeted me ignoring an introduction to the two strangers. They had lowered their voices a little but their conversation 71 was still – I am sure – audible to others at nearby tables and turning to one of them – I said – "You guys should soft pedal a little – you don't know who is riding the Erie – maybe you don't care – but please keep it quiet – while I'm on the scene – I don't want a bust nor can I stand a frisk – I got a stick of pot in my pocket." Without being too concerned with the effect this had on them – I turned to Frenchy – showing him the gloves – which he said he didn't want – to keep them – all he was interested in was jewelry. Finishing my coffee – I nodded to the two cats – said – "be seeing you" – to Frenchy then walked out onto the street – cutting toward 8th Avenue – and met a cat from the Village who laid a buck on me – asking, "Is there a connection around, man? I have to cop. I'm alright, but my old lady is getting sick. It's too early to see my man." I told him – "Nothing happening man." He was heading toward 7th Avenue and I joined him until – reaching the subway – he said "I split here – take it easy – so long."

I continued on until I reached the Bryant movie house where on the spur of the moment I decided to go in and see the picture – meanwhile staying out of the cold – killing a few hours till later in the day when things would in all probability be a little more active. I had just settled comfortably in my seat – glancing to my right – in the row of seats immediately in front of me I looked directly into the face of the darker complexioned fellow who had been sitting talking with Frenchy. He smiled – leaned toward me and sotto voce asked if I would mind him joining me. I replied "not at all man – great." We sat next to each other thru the picture until the end – not speaking much. Once when he said – "my name is Johnnie – Johnnie Terrell – what's yours?" – I told him my name – "Herb Huncke – call me Huncke." He looked at me – smiled a little and said "man – what a crazy name." At the end of the film he suggested we leave – asking if I would like to get some coffee – and if I still had the joint of pot. I answered yes to both questions. We left walking up 42nd Street to 6th Avenue around the corner into the 6th Avenue Automat.

We sat at one of the front tables – up near the window – watching the people rushing past – glancing at the park – 72 observing the back of the public library – commenting now and then about the passing automobiles. He asked me about New York – what I thought of it – did it really swing – once apropos of nothing he said – "I dig the way you comb your hair." Oddly enough – I had been thinking about his hair – which had one wave in the front carefully pushed into place – was long and combed into a precise duck-ass in back – laughing at his remark, said – "As a matter of fact – I dig yours" – and we both laughed.

His general appearance was engaging. He was about 5'8" in height – slim – with well developed shoulders tapering to a narrow waist. His facial features were sharply shaped – his mouth well formed with warm red lips – his nose small with gently flaring nostrils and his deep brown eyes tending toward almond shape – giving him a rather oriental look – heightened somewhat by an olive coloring. He was like a mischievous angel might appear.

Unexpectedly he said – "will you be my partner? I'm lonely and need a friend – I want you for my friend." There was something so direct and appealing in the manner in which he made the request – I suddenly felt a new stirring of life in me – as though I was being awakened after a long slumber. I felt good – yet at the same time I was filled with a feeling of shame – what right had I to come close to a young angel – what could I bring into a relationship of any kind but death and pollution – I was sick, sick, sick. I began trying to explain – "I'm broke, man – I haven't even a place to live – the only clothes I own I'm wearing. I can't take care of myself – how can I possibly be of any help to you? I'm not even a good has-been. Man, you would be better off to stay away from me." He looked at me – even more intently than when he had been watching earlier – saying "forget it man – just be my friend. I have a little money and you know your way around – between the two of us we'll both get straight. Don't worry – I like you man – I think you're good people – come on – let's go somewhere and light up the joint."

It was a strange sensation – like suddenly regaining a purpose. After discussing his friend – they had both come to New York from Detroit – his buddy was going to continue on to Virginia to see relatives – there would be no difficulty.

He had a few dollars and we checked into the William Sloane House Y.M.C.A. on 34th Street – which began a 73 strange friendship. He was a great cat – helped give me back a desire to live. Our knowing each other was a great experience. He taught me how to burglarize – making it a sort of adventure – rather exciting. Eventually we split up. I heard – indirectly – he is serving a big bit in Michigan State Prison.

JOHNNIE II

We had checked into the Sloane House Y.M.C.A. during the afternoon. I was completely broke and Johnnie had taken one of his suits to the pawn shop. The afternoon passed quickly. We had sat talking for several hours. Johnnie had told me of himself and of Detroit – how he had decided to come to New York. He was interested in the theater – liked show business and had met a few celebrities – one whom he intended looking up at the Capitol Theater where he was blowing with a name band (Glenn Miller's old band) – that perhaps someday he would get into show business – maybe become a singer or even an actor. He also spoke of his father whom he loved but who didn't understand him. He wanted him to get a job – any kind of job – bus boy – dishwasher – something. His father simply couldn't understand he just wasn't cut out to work in a restaurant. He wanted to work but life was still a big adventure – after all, who knows, perhaps he would meet a woman he would fall in love with and she would be rich and they would travel all over the world. Maybe go to China – or Tibet – or India – would hunt tigers – ride elephants – sail down the Congo – smoke opium – discover a diamond mine – collect rare paintings – have sharp clothes – really live. Then also there was the possibility of becoming a revolutionary – somewhere in the Latin American countries – being the leader or at least the leader's righthand man. Besides there was deep-sea fishing – voodoo – unexplored jungles – mountains to climb – fortunes to be won at the gambling tables in Cannes. Man – there is just too much happening in the world to get stuck in some two-bit job not paying enough to live on. He asked me if I knew anything about getting seaman's papers – explaining a friend of his had gone to sea during the war and made a lot of money and liked the sea. He thought it would be great going to sea. I told him I already had my seaman's papers – that we would hit downtown the next day and see what could be done. We made plans for the 75 next few days – discussing all the places we might go if he could get his papers. Suddenly he looked at me and repeated what he had said when we first became acquainted – "I like you man – you're fine."

We weren't exactly sure what we were going to do concerning the immediate problem of obtaining money but it didn't seem to worry Johnnie and I was still close to death – aware of being alive once again – absorbed by a consciousness of no longer being alone – afraid still to believe in the miracle of being loved – amazed at my laughter – unable to accept – simply – friendship – to think in practical terms of making a daily living – only resolving to make every effort to keep Johnnie near and close to me.

The day had been cold and crisp – the evening was bright and clear – the sky filled with stars. We had stopped by the room – taken showers – dressed in some of Johnnie's clothes – each wearing leather jackets – his black, mine brown – Spanish pegged trousers (my first pair) – sport shirts fastened at the collar – leather gloves – and hats pushed back on our heads, the brims snapped down in front. We hadn't discussed what we would do. I sort of permitted Johnnie to make the decisions and thought it a great idea when he suggested – it being so beautiful a night – that we ride the Staten Island Ferry – get off in Staten Island and take a long walk.

The ride on the subway was fun – Johnnie pretending part of the time he was deaf and dumb, talking with his fingers, smiling at people – laughing at me because I didn't catch on quick enough and became embarrassed when I tried to play his game with him, becoming clumsy with my fingers. Motioning finally for me to join him on the front platform of the subway car where for the rest of the ride he recited make-believe poetry – becoming dramatic – waving his arms around – exclaiming in heavy resonant tones. He was the knight of old – come to save the maiden in distress – to slay the dragon – to fight duels – to ride off into the night on a black stallion. Aboard the ferry boat we stood out in the cold wind in the front pretending to be Vikings – setting sail for distant ports – prepared to discover new lands, new people. Gazing back now and then at the sparkling beauty of New York looming against the night sky –

hailing the Statue of Liberty – shouting Ahoy! to the passengers aboard the ferry passing en route to New York – grinning at the disapproving countenances of several of our fellow riders. Johnnie put his arm around my shoulder saying – "This is real fine man. All New York right here before me. When I feel this good nothing can go wrong." He began singing – imitating Frank Sinatra.

Upon arrival in Staten Island we disembarked. Johnnie was leading the way – still singing – stopping now and then to comment about some passing stranger – flirting with several young girls rushing toward the ferry who began laughing among themselves – leaning a bit closer together whispering – tossing their heads – pretending to be indifferent.

We walked along one of the streets bordering the waterfront – looking at New York – coming to a standstill once while Johnnie opened his arms wide as though to gather in the whole scene – slowly closing them and asking me if I could imagine what it must have looked like to the first settlers when it was still a wilderness – an island of forests belonging to the Indians – teeming with wildlife – birds – all kinds of wild animals – deer, rabbit, fox, bear. He said he would like to have been alive then and have discovered the one particular spot which is Manhattan. He said – "It's great now – but it must have been even greater then. Man – if I had been there I'd have arranged to keep it just as it was – no big buildings – no automobiles – only a few people, carefully selected. Think man – when you were hungry, there was the river – or you could hunt and you could have a small garden and grow all kinds of vegetables. You could have had a little house – and a fireplace and at night you would have sat around talking – telling stories – or strumming a guitar and singing. Wow – man – it sure would have been great.

We continued walking – gradually leaving the waterfront behind – until we reached a somewhat prosperous residential section – located in rather hilly terrain – with houses scattered here and there on the sides of the hills. It was still early in the evening and we could see people eating their dinners. Most of the houses were lit up but occasionally we would pass one that was dark – the owners away – perhaps visiting friends or taking in the theater in New York. At one point we reached the top of a hill with a house situated in a grove of trees about halfway down the side when Johnnie turned to me and said – "Have you ever broken into a house?"

ED LEARY

I hadn't been in New York long when I met Eddie. When I first arrived I was stone broke and like every young kid who hits New York broke I went directly to 42nd Street. I hadn't known anything about 42nd Street but the name – nevertheless there I went – in no time becoming hip to the hustling routine – getting by fairly easily – meeting all kinds of people – having experiences I had never suspected possible. I soon became acquainted with many of the regular habitués – one night getting disgustingly drunk with a kid who was going on his second year as a 42nd Street hustler – doing a little stealing on the side – taking me along on this particular occasion – showing me how to break into automobiles – stealing such items as suitcases, topcoats, suits or anything of value left in the car – and because we were drunk and hardly realizing what we were doing, we got caught – each of us ending up serving six months on Rikers Island. This was my first prison experience and although in many respects unpleasant – at the same time interesting. When we were released we went right back to 42nd Street.

At the corner of 8th Avenue and 42nd Street there used to be a notorious bar where petty crooks – fags – hustlers and people of every description hung out – known as the Bucket of Blood – although that wasn't the real name. Someone would say – "Man, I've got to cut out now – I'll pick you up later at the Bucket of Blood" – and you knew where he meant. I guess every city has its Bucket of Blood because I have run into several of them all over the country.

The first night following my release I went into the Bucket of Blood and met Eddie. I had been standing at the bar – looking the crowd over and nursing a glass of beer – when from out of nowhere he came over and spoke to me. He said "Hi – would you like to have a drink with me?" I answered "Sure – why not." He told me to go ahead and order a shot of whiskey and to forget the beer. He said he had been watching me for some time and figured I was 79 probably broke and could use a couple of drinks. The place was exceptionally crowded with people – pushing and milling around the bar – the juke box blasting some popular record. The whole room was filled with smoke – the overhead fluorescent light filtering through giving the place an eerie quality. The shouting and talking deafened one – mixed with the blaring sounds of music – the general atmosphere was like a small slice of hell. Eddie said he had seen me before – asking me to guess where he had seen me. I named a few places around the square. Each time he shook his head smiling – at last saying "It was in jail – over on the Island. I used to watch you in the mess hall at chow time. Your company went in ahead of mine. I noticed how you always kept yourself looking pretty sharp – your hair always combed just so – you stood out from the others around yu. I tried to meet you but somehow it never worked out. I figured you might hang around the square.

Eddie's appearance was good-looking in the sense he bore himself with quiet dignity – conservatively – with the suggestion of an inner turbulence threatening to come to the surface were he to relax – piquing my curiosity – giving me the impression of depth. His coloring was medium light. His facial features finely drawn – somewhat sharp and pointed – his eyes gray from within full of light – his mouth thin and well shaped. His hair was wavy – streaked silver-gray – of which he was exceedingly conscious. He was about twenty-eight at the time I am speaking of – and first he was sure his hair made him appear old – then he was sure it was conspicuous or it made him look effeminate.

We stood talking at the bar a long time – getting a little drunk – telling each other about ourselves – our plans, our experiences, how we had gotten into trouble, into jail – finally one or the other mentioned narcotics. He told me he had first started using heroin or H while in the army in Panama. At that time he used stuff for a period of about eighteen months until he ran into some difficulty with a girl he was shacking up with – who in a fit of jealousy – as I remember the story – reported him to the army authorities – causing him to be dishonorably discharged after being sent to the stockade – where he served almost three years. 80 He returned to his beloved Brooklyn – staying off stuff –

getting a job as a trolley driver – until one night about two years before we met he pulled into the car barn, stepped down off his car into the path of a car pulling into the barn – was hit – receiving a broken leg. While convalescing he became involved with a male nurse who would occasionally supply him with morphine and he was soon hooked.

I told him of my own experience with junk in Chicago. Of how along with a friend of mine I had started picking up on heroin – finally getting mildly hooked – having to kick when my only source of supply had been arrested and sent to jail. I explained I was pretty green about the whole routine and that when it became necessary to kick – I went to my mother – who had been very upset – but had sensibly helped me by taking me to her doctor, who had given me a reduction cure. I told him it had been an unpleasant experience, but I had actually not had too much trouble and that it had happened about three years ago.

During our conversation we both discovered that we were still interested in junk and that we both preferred it to drinking. I mentioned knowing a pot connection who might be around although I hadn't seen him since getting out of jail – that I liked smoking pot – we called it gauge or tea in those days – and perhaps if we looked around we could find him. Eddie said he didn't like smoking it – that he didn't like the kick. He felt if one was going to smoke it should be the pipe – opium. He did suggest maybe the guy would know where to score some H – asking me if I would like to shoot a little stuff.

We had another drink at the bar discussing what we would do if we did score. I told him – as he had guessed I was stone broke without even a place to sleep – had come into the joint intending to try and pick up a queen, score for some loot and get a place to stay. Eddie said not to worry about that – if I wanted to I could check into a hotel with him – he was planning to stay over in New York for a couple of days anyway – besides he liked me and this would give us an opportunity to get to know each other better – also he was anxious by now to get some stuff and get on. I had taken an immediate liking to Eddie and this plan suited me fine.

Shortly after leaving the Bucket of Blood, along 8th

Avenue between 45th Street and 46th Street we located Hugh the pot connection and asked him to make a heroin score for us. As it happened he had recently run into some fellow uptown while picking up his supply of pot – who had suggested he might run into some of his customers anxious to cop some stuff and to get in touch with him – he could get him as much as he wanted. Stuff was being pushed in capsules at the time and we asked Hugh to pick up two. Eddie and I had decided to check into a small hotel at 51st Street and 8th Avenue where I had stayed a few times before being arrested. I was sure we could get a room without difficulty. We arranged to meet Hugh in the coffee shop on the same corner in an hour.

Eddie and I continued up the Avenue until we reached the hotel where we rented a room for a week – Eddie having decided at the last minute – since he was holding fairly heavy financially – he might as well stake me to a room for a week – also it would give him a place to fall in should he return to the city sooner than he expected.

While we were waiting for Hugh to get back we cut down the street to a drugstore – where I used to be able to buy anything short of the real McCoy – benzedrine, seconal, nembutal – any of the barbiturates – eyedroppers and hypodermic needles. We bought two droppers and a couple of spikes – needles – No. 26-half inch and some wires for cleaning them. We stopped in the Automat for coffee and before leaving picked up two teaspoons.

We had been doing a lot of talking – feeling each other out about our likes and dislikes – and as I learned more about Eddie the greater became my interest in him. Although I had met thieves and hustlers and knock-around characters of all kinds in the past couple of years Eddie was the first I met who lived by his wits – impressing me as being competent and capable of carrying out plans. He was definitely intelligent and carried himself with what is generally termed – in the vernacular of the underworld – class. There was a certain evilness about him which appealed to me although – much later – I came to realize the evilness I saw in Eddie – and this was true in Eddie's case particularly – was mostly projection on my part. Oddly enough Eddie

recognized this much sooner than I did – allowing me to

relax – and to display what could be called voraciousness and lack of inhibitions with him I never attained before or since with anyone else.

We met Hugh on time and he asked to come along with us – he said he had never tried stuff and wanted to – he'd heard so much about it he wanted to find out if it was as great as everyone said. The three of us went up to the room and turned on. It didn't take much to get us high – neither Eddie or me had used for quite some time and it was Hugh's first experience. We all three got really stoned and sat talking or simply going on the nod until the early hours of the morning – finally dropping off to sleep – awakening much later in the day. We all three felt fairly good although somewhat sluggish. Hugh lit up a couple of sticks of pot before cutting out – leaving us feeling good and a bit high. After Hugh left, Eddie and I split what was left of the stuff.

Eddie was an entirely new type of person to me. I had never known anyone like him nor for that matter have I since met anyone his equal in independence and scheming know-how. He wasn't vicious or cruel in any sense – yet at the same time he was completely devoid of sentiment. He spoke in detail of his past life but never once mentioned having any feeling of love for anyone he had known and spoke of his family in an offhand detached manner. He had lived with several women but seemingly missed none of them and spoke of having left each one in the way one might speak of discarding an old suit or piece of clothing one has grown weary of. Yet – and this is what attracted me particularly – there was a certain warmth and immediate concern for – in this instance – my feelings, permeating his conversation and dealings with me – not only at the time but for as long as we were closely associated. There were very pronounced homosexual characteristics in his personality – he permitted himself indulgence in it with me – so that in a sense strong feelings of love existed between us – although he carefully avoided its becoming obvious to any of our mutual acquaintances, as well as refusing to acknowledge it even when we were alone in words – only in physical fact. He did say at one time that I was the only male he had ever allowed himself such complete freedom with. During our discussion prior to going downstairs for 83 breakfast – we had decided it would be great to try and score again – later in the evening. We had talked about the money situation and Eddie had come up with a plan. Shortly before we had been sent over to the Island there had been a big drive on against the junk pushers. San Juan Hill – a notorious cesspool of crime and corruption of all kinds where – if one was at all known, one could cop any kind of junk from ordinary sleeping pills to opium – had finally been cleaned up. For a long time the police had been unable to move in on the district. It was actually a little world – set apart – controlled entirely by the underworld element. Just how they had accomplished cleaning it up was rather a mystery – but clean it up they did – along with the Lower East Side, Broadway and various other spots. A panic was on among the junkies. There were still a few people able to connect – but on the whole conditions were bad. A little of all this I already knew but Eddie was well informed about the details. He spoke of having run into a Broadway whore he knew – who had told him most of the girls were finding the going rough – unable to score regularly – and were willing to pay almost any amount of money to make a steady connection. Eddie explained he knew of several doctors in Brooklyn who – if given the right approach – would write prescriptions for five grains of morphine. He had it figured between the two of us we could score enough from these doctors to keep ourselves supplied – the rest we could sell to the girls along Broadway. He said – "We'll pick about five customers – steady and dependable – and promise to keep them supplied regularly." The plan struck me as excellent – although I had some doubts about my ability to convince the doctors to write. Eddie told me not to worry – he would tell me exactly what to say and with my appearance I'd have no trouble at all. This wasn't exactly an original plan with Eddie. He told me he knew of a couple of people who were keeping up habits making croakers. In fact later it became so common the government men began cracking down on the doctors – taking a number of them to court for illicitly writing prescriptions – all of them losing their licenses to practice medicine and many of them ending up serving time. We got into the racket at the right time and had almost a two-year run before getting into trouble.

We spent the remainder of the day wandering around Times Square – Eddie introduced me to a couple of the whores he knew who said they were willing to do business with us – if we could promise a steady thing. They weren't particularly interested in morphine – since they had heroin habits – but figured the situation had reached the place where as long as they could depend on at least a daily meet, in the long run they would be better off making the switch. We did a lot of window shopping. In those days I was still clothes-conscious – picking out shirts – suits – shoes – and all kinds of haberdashery. Eddie considered himself a sharp dresser and he was. Late in the evening we cut into Hugh and picked up two more caps. He told us his man was hot and didn't like doing business in such small amounts. He said his man had told him he was trying to get rid of what he had left in one drop – about an ounce – so unless we wanted to take the whole thing we had better look for someone else. We explained we had other plans. Hugh half wanted to come along with us but we said we had business to discuss and we'd pick up some other time. The two of us returned to the room – got straight – Eddie then proceeding to instruct me in how to go about scoring with a doctor.

Actually the routine was fairly simple. My approach consisted of telling the doctor – with lowered eyes, hesitant speech and seeming humiliation – I was a drug addict – having picked up the habit while visiting in Florida with my people. We had traveled through the Everglades and I had developed a severe colitis condition accompanied by amoebic dysentery – the doctor giving me morphine to ease the pain. This was the general outline of my story – except that I also explained further to the doctor that the doctor who had treated me since I returned to New York had recently passed on and I didn't like or feel comfortable with the man who had taken over his practice. It worked and the next day the first doctor over in Brooklyn Eddie recommended wrote for five grains of morphine without giving me any trouble. Eddie had waited down the block for me and as soon as I came out – he went in. His story was considerably different from mine – having to do mostly with his accident in the car barn and his leg not having healed properly. The same day we each made three doctors. One of them we simply hit on 85 by chance passing his office – deciding to go in and try him. The other two – Eddie said – had been suggested to him by some guy he had met in jail. Getting the prescriptions filled was no problem since they were legitimate – a doctor had written them. We received vials – government sealed with twenty quarter-grain tablets for each script – giving us a total of thirty grains of morphine at the end of our afternoon's work. The prescriptions had cost around three dollars apiece and getting them filled averaged one dollar and a half to a dollar seventy-five. Our cash outlay amounted to almost twenty-five dollars plus personal expense – coming to roughly five or six dollars. That evening the two girls – along with a friend of theirs – bought all but three grains – at one dollar a quarter grain. Morphine sold or pushed on the street cost four dollars per grain. We were moderately successful and soon did a steady business – with four, occasionally five, regular customers – Broadway whores – with a net profit of about one hundred dollars a day. Eddie proved an excellent manager of money – although we both steadily increased our own habits, cutting down the actual financial gain. One whore alone – a large wholesome good-looking woman named Sal – did forty to forty-five dollars worth of business with us. She was a good money-maker and we could always count on hearing from her – two or three times each evening. She became a good friend – frequently coming to see us – sitting talking or shooting up – taking a rest in between her working periods. She was remarkable in that she showed absolutely none of the effects of the usual drug addict. She continued to remain large and healthy-appearing with bright natural coloring. She was a heavy eater, smoked incessantly and shot up no less than ten grains of morphine each day. She was amazingly good natured – seldom indulging in self-pity – never gossiping and always anxious to help anyone. She set aside a few dollars every day – for handouts to some of her less fortunate sisters or for the innumerable Times Square characters she knew out scuffling around trying to score one way or another. She had a young daughter somewhere – with someone – whom she supported. She loved her deeply and never failed – when occasionally the three of us went out for something to eat – often Chinatown – to pick up some trinket to surprise her with.

Our business venture had proven successful and we began laying money aside for a trip the following spring to California. The holidays came and went and one day we realized we had been together almost a year. It seemed incredible. A whole year had passed with things going along smoothly – a record for both of us. In the beginning Eddie had been a bit self-conscious of our relationship but even that had ceased to be of importance and he now no longer considered it strange. We were unexcitably happy. We had our arguments and sudden flare-ups of temper – but thus far nothing really serious. Eddie had gotten rather melancholy around the holidays but it had passed quickly.

Most of the doctors we had started with were still with us. One suddenly had trouble with the law over an abortion case he was involved in and another had gotten cold feet after some junkies he had been writing scripts for took a fall – mentioning his name to the police who had promptly paid him a visit – refusing thereafter to write any more for anyone. As for the rest – about six in all – most were not only writing prescriptions for us in our own names but would also – for an extra few dollars – write scripts with other names which they would readily honor when questioned by the pharmacist. There were several druggists as well – we had gotten to know who would always fill our scripts without question.

Most of our doctors were located in Brooklyn. One afternoon I had made a trip over to Brooklyn alone – in order to pick up an extra script from a doctor who had been with us almost from the first. Eddie planned on seeing someone else – the two of us expecting to see each other back at our place late in the afternoon. It was a beautiful day – all golden and full of sunshine with the first hint of warm weather.

I had seen the doctor – incidentally picking up on a quarter-grain fix before leaving his office – returned to New York – stopped by a drugstore – had the script filled – stepped out onto the street and was just getting ready to cross over to the other side, when I was suddenly gripped on the arm by a neatly-dressed, unassuming-appearing young man who – before I realized what was actually happening – reached 87 into my pocket, removed the box of morphine tablets and said, "Step over here – I want to speak with you" – flashed a badge and further added – "Federal agent." I was so completely taken by surprise it was several minutes before I became conscious of just why I was being stopped. He was very polite asking me about the box of morphine – inquiring whether I was an addict or not and if so how long had I been an addict – but particularly how long this particular doctor had been taking care of me. He went on further to explain there had been a number of prescriptions written in his name. I answered his questions as honestly as possible without admitting the doctor had long known I was simply a drug addict and was merely doing business with me. He then asked me to step back into the drugstore – while he checked further with the druggist who assured him the script was legitimate – having called the doctor to make sure. He and the druggist spoke in undertones together for a few minutes. He then turned to me and told me I could go – giving me back the morphine at the same time. I departed as quickly as possible. I used a somewhat roundabout way of returning home – feeling pretty sure at the same time the man undoubtedly already knew where I lived. When I got in Eddie still hadn't returned. I called the doctor immediately – describing in detail exactly what had happened – advising him to lay off writing scripts for a while at least. A short time later Eddie returned and I gave him a full account of what had taken place. Eddie was calm about the whole thing – saying only, "Well, man, that's the end of another good doctor." We discussed to some extent whether or not we would be wise to move, finally deciding in favor of staying – figuring if we were due for trouble we'd get it whether we moved or not. Eddie did make other arrangements with our customers about meets, etc. But otherwise we continued along pretty much as we had been. We never did have any further trouble directly as a result of this particular episode but it did act as a turning point in our general good luck.

Shortly afterward one of our dependable sources of supply began getting nervous and cut us down to one script apiece a week. Almost the same thing happened with a doctor we had recently contacted. All of them were getting jumpy. Several arrests had been made of doctors in New York – and the papers had played the cases up big. We were becomming increasingly worried – having had to cut out one of our customers already because of being unable to get hold of enough stuff steadily to take care of our own habits and handle the usual number of customers as well. We began looking round for new doctors – covering neighborhoods we had previously shied clear of. Then one day we solved the situation – we decided to write our own scripts. In the same way our first plan wasn't original, this plan wasn't either. We both were conscious of the bigger risk involved – but we were also aware we were caught up in a situation we had to contend with – no matter what else happened. The whole junk scene – insofar as the user was concerned – was growing worse instead of better. Junkies were becoming desperate – more and more of them turning to crimes of violence in order to keep up their habits. The stuff being pushed on the streets was becoming more expensive and harder to get. There had always been a certain amount of criminal action involved with junk, but prior to this period it had been kept somewhat to a minimum. Now anything went. Also – and what is probably the strangest aspect of the whole deal – more and more people were taking an interest in junk – becoming curious about it – experimenting with it. The idea was if you handled junk – automatically you made money.

Eddie and myself were fortunate in that we were pretty well organized and although our immediate predicament was unpleasant, we felt our new solution would be effective. And it was.

We spent one afternoon going around to doctors' offices – choosing times we were fairly sure they weren't in – picking doctors in most instances whose offices were in their homes – asking permission of whoever answered our knock to await the doctor's return – gaining access to their offices – stealing the prescription blanks – usually somewhere on top of the desk – calling whoever had let us in – saying we had changed our minds and would call later. We worked separately. Eddie picked up three script pads and I managed to get hold of two. That evening – choosing again a time we were sure the doctor would be out – usually calling 89 his phone number to make sure – after simply copying a prescription we filled in our stolen blanks – about three of them – went to the drugstore and had them filled without trouble. This system worked splendidly – although once in a while a druggist would become suspicious and suggest we return later.

We worked out a rather cool procedure for filling them out – taking names from the telephone directory listed in the vicinity of the drugstores we had planned on hitting that day. Eddie would write the scripts one day – going along to keep me company – waiting outside until I'd come out – and the next day I'd write the scripts and Eddie would get them filled.

Our life together was still going smoothly, but an almost imperceptible tension underlying our everyday activities had crept in. We were beginning to ever so slowly draw apart. It was noticable in little things. We had always sort of made a ritual of shooting up together – now sometimes we wouldn't wait for each other. We had always enjoyed going places together – now we started cutting out alone. We began seeing more people – occasionally one of us leaving with one of our visitors – taking in a show alone – splitting from the scene without saying when we'd get back – arguing more frequently and with lesser provocation.

Meanwhile – Phil White came back on the scene. I had found him in the beginning an interesting person so when he began coming around inviting us out or up to his place to pick up on music and maybe smoke a little pot and keep him and his old lady company – Eddie would decline and I would go along. Phil had just gotten settled with the woman he was living with – whose whole background was a pseudo-respectable set-up which she clung to tenaciously – being attracted to Phill primarily because he represented a side of life she secretly felt part of. She was supporting Phill at the time and he felt duty bound to spend much of his time with her. He liked taking me to their place because he could relax and be himself while at the same time confident I wouldn't do anything to jeopardize his position with Kay.

I don't think Eddie was jealous of my interest in Phil – but he resented him – telling me Phil was unworthy of any sincere friendship and basically a fool and a phony. He admitted having had business dealings with Phil but assured me Phil was not to be trusted.

Then one afternoon we got the news Sal had been arrested. We both felt badly and Eddie went down to the women's prison to try and bail her out. She was a multiple offender and they had set bail at fifteen hundred, which we didn't have. She had become so much a part of our daily life we felt the loss greatly. It turned out it was the last I was to see of her for many years. I ran into her about five years ago. She was looking much the same – a little heavier, perhaps – of course older – but surprisingly no longer on junk – married – happily getting ready for her daughter's graduation from high school. We talked a while – reminiscing over the past – wondering about Eddie.

New York was exceedingly hot that summer. The heat settled down over the city in a huge blanket. The days were long and humid and nobody was any more active than was absolutely necessary. Somehow we got through the summer – sleeping late in the day – getting up – cashing our scripts – taking care of business – lying around or making Central Park. Eddie had started going back to Brooklyn and began talking about moving over there sometime during the autumn. I was a little hesitant about committing myself to such a move mostly because I felt it would only complicate our set-up.

September came and the early fall rains. I purchased an umbrella and frequently carried my extra scripts folded inside. We no longer went out together to cash scripts.

It had been raining all day and was beginning to clear up. We had both slept late and Eddie awakened feeling disagreeable. It was my afternoon to go out and while Eddie wrote out scripts, I got dressed. I had bought a new fall suit I liked and although it still looked like more rain decided in favor of wearing it. I affected very conservative attire at the time because – principally – I was working the East Side and felt it wiser to be as inconspicuous as possible. I wore a neat white shirt and tie and with my umbrella hanging from my arm – my new suit and a hat – looked presumably the height of respectability.

There was a sudden heavy downpour as I came out of the building. I hailed a cab and was driven to the East Side 91 to the approximate location of one of the stores I had anticipated using. I presented my prescription and was told to wait. The pharmacist returned in a moment saying, "I am sorry but I can't fill your prescription – we are completely out of quarter-grain tablets." Had it been a less unpleasant day, weatherwise, I wouldn't have minded quite as much as I did. I could simply have ignored the entire district and moved on to the next location of my prearranged schedule – later if necessary returning home and making out new scripts for a different neighborhood. Since it was so bad – I decided to go to a drugstore a short distance away I had been to on at least three previous occasions. There were several drugstores most cooperative, and I had added this one to the list. My reasoning being – the druggist had known after my first visit to him that my scripts were phony – surely having checked with the doctor at his first opportunity, and if not after the first time certainly the second time I had come in. By this time the late afternoon commuters were beginning to pour into Grand Central. Many of them were in the store – located almost across the street from one of the entrances to the station – making last-minute purchases of toilet articles etc. Therefore when I presented my script to one of the clerks – one I had spoken with before – he on this occasion greeted me pleasantly – inquiring of my general welfare – apologizing, due to the rushing business, for my having to wait – assuring me I would be taken care of as quickly as possible. There are two entrance ways to this particular store – it is still in the same location and I have been in it many times since – and I was taken by complete surprise when, after having waited only a few minutes, I looked up to see two uniformed policemen rapidly approaching by way of one entrance – at the same time realizing two of the men pushing through the crowd of shoppers toward me from the other entrance were plain-clothes detectives. Both sets of police reached me simultaneously – grabbing me on both sides – pulling me in both directions – beginning to argue immediately as to who had gotten to me first and shuld receive credit for making the arrest. It was both tragic and humorous. Finally while creating a great scene of capturing a narcotic addict – implying I was dangerous – pointing a gun at me – telling me to stand still – not to make a move

92

– both pairs towering over me in height – frisking me – grabbing my umbrella – one of them loudly saying, "None of that," as though I had intended using it as a weapon – pushing me toward the doorway – telling people to step aside – out into the street where a huge crowd of people had gathered – peering and grimacing at me – some laughing – asking questions – others looking at me as though I were the scum of the earth – some with amazement to see a real live criminal.

They were still arguing as to who was to take me to the station – peering down at me – leaning over closer to me asking – "Which of us got here first?" I decided in favor of the detectives, thinking in all probability they would be easier to get along with than a couple of promotion-conscious harness cops. I chose wisely. They turned out to be fairly decent – even arranging to get me a fix later when I began getting really sick. I was booked and charged with attempting to obtain narcotics through fraud – a misdemeanor – and eventually sentenced to another six months on Riker's Island. I kept Eddie's name out of it – not giving them my proper address – telling them that my only possessions were those I had with me – that I had been making it playing cards and shooting craps – had not used drugs for long – that I had been living in the Mills Hotel paying by the night. They asked me about the scripts and I told them I had bought them from a guy on the corner of 43rd Street and 8th Avenue – one of the kids from 42nd Street pointed him out to me – that I didn't even know his name and wasn't sure I would recognize him were we to come face to face. They didn't believe me but there was nothing they could do about it.

While I was away Eddie corresponded with me regularly, sending money for cigarettes and a few of the necessities – such as a toothbrush – toothpaste – soap and candy. Candy is a must when a junky kicks a habit. He kept me informed to some extent of his activities. Much of what was happening to him I had to guess from the well-known reading between the lines. Sal had finally been sent away for a year – another of the girls had taken a fall – there had been some difficulty at home concerning someone who had come to visit us drunk and disorderly and Eddie had been 93 asked to move. He was finding the going rough – and missed me. By the time of my discharge Eddie had gone back to Brooklyn. What he failed to mention was he had – just before moving to Brooklyn – acquired a new partner.

When I got out I went directly to the Brooklyn address. Instead of Eddie opening the door, Georgie, his new partner, opened it – saying "Hello – Ed isn't home just yet. We have been expecting you. I hope you will like me. Eddie thinks we all three can get along real great. He had told me what a swell guy you are." Georgie was a nice person but perhaps jealousy caused me to resent him and to decide against any plans in which the three of us were to be involved. Georgie had some stuff stashed away and before Eddie got in gave me a little fix. Eddie arrived all smiles and good will – telling me how much he had missed me – how bad he had felt when he realized – when I didn't come home the night of the pinch – what must have happened. Georgie had something to do and excused himself saying – "You two will have a lot to talk about – I'll see you both later." As soon as Georgie left, Eddie came over to me, put his arms around me and said – "Man I've missed you so much – I never thought it could happen – anyone could come to mean as much to me as you do." He explained things had gotten pretty bad financially and that he had originally decided to double up with Georgie to save on expenses, but since living with him he had grown to like him. He said he was sure I could understand and that Georgie being there wouldn't make any difference to our friendship. He had it figured the three of us could reorganize our original set-up – living in Brooklyn this time but still doing business in New York. He went on to explain he had made some new contracts and we could with the third party do even better than when there had been just him and me. I told him it all sounded great but somehow I didn't like it – also said I wasn't sure I liked Georgie.

The section of Brooklyn Eddie and Georgie had settled in is known as Bay Ridge, and although I stayed there only a short time I liked it. A good number of people living in the district are of Scandinavian descent – many going to sea. The bars in the neighborhood cater to seamen and there is a certain air of the romantic and adventurous. Eddie had discovered several Swedish eating places we frequented often – the three of us creating a strange appearance in our sharp clothes and somewhat obvious disregard of the staid conservative manner of our neighbors. We came and went at all hours of the day and night. It was apparent none of us worked legitimately – still we were never made to feel uncomfortable or treated as outsiders – the principle of live and let live seemingly the opinion of most of the people we came in contact with. The apartment was spacious and comfortably furnished – but I felt a strangeness with Georgie I was unable to overcome and began thinking about leaving.

We settled to a routine satisfactory to the three of us – each of us assuming certain responsibilities of our own. It worked well enough and perhaps we could have continued indefinitely. Somehow though I was uncomfortable with Georgie. I was jealous of the attention Eddie directed toward him – becoming angry on the slightest pretext – finally telling Georgie I didn't like him – considered him weak and ineffectual – stupid and a bore – and that I was going to clear out. Eddie grew angry, accusing me of being unkind and unfair – telling me if I didn't apologize to Georgie I had better make arrangements to live somewhere else. It was true – I had been unfair and I knew it – but it was impossible for me to apologize.

We did spend our last few days together happily, but when I succeeded in locating a room in Manhattan I was relieved to get away. It was fine to once again be alone. We continued seeing each other daily – making the doctors – occasionally falling into a movie – or going to Chinatown for food. It wasn't long until I began meeting new people – and frequently when Ed and Georgie would suggest our going somewhere together I would already have other plans.

And so we gradually drifted apart. I found new sources of supply for junk – beginning to cop uptown in Harlem. Eventually I failed to keep appointments with Ed and Georgie and it followed that soon thereafter I stopped seeing them altogether.

One day, running into a mutual friend, I learned Georgie had been arrested and Ed had gone to the Hospital in Kentucky to kick his habit.

Several years passed and one day I ran into Ed. We

were both pleased to see each other but neither of us had any desire to become involved in close association. We talked and reminisced – shot up a couple of bags of heroin – spending the night in a Times Square hotel. Next day – Ed had plans of his own and so did I. We parted good friends.

Up till three years ago, periodically we would meet – sit and talk – and once I went back over to Brooklyn with him and stayed over the weekend. Georgie had disappeared completely and I have never run into him.

I never see Ed anymore and can't pick up any news of him. Every now and then I'll meet someone who remembers us as a team and we'll discuss the good old days. Everyone remembers Ed with good feeling.

It is possible I'll see him again – although in my heart I feel he might be dead.

Looking back over our friendship it occurs to me Ed Leary influenced my life in all probability more than anyone else I've known.

SEA VOYAGE

Phil awakened me early in the morning – apparently Bozo let him in – pulling the bedclothes off and exposing me to a biting cold draft from the open window. Bob and I had shared the studio couch in the front room and we had drawn together during the night to keep warm and I had wrapped my arms around him – something that I secretly wanted to do – and it was with added reluctance I greeted Phil who stood hovering over the couch sort of clucking with a widespread leer on his face. It was from a pleasant drowsiness and peaceful dream I awakened into the nightmare morning.

A cold chilling wind whined outside the windows and the sky was overladen with grey clouds. Cold city sounds carried up from the streets and there was nothing I wanted quite so much as to remain in bed.

Kay and Phil had recently been quarreling – Kay complaining about Phil's habit and pleading with him to try and kick and finally suggesting that he and I get a job aboard a ship together so that we both might kick. Phil in order to restore peace and partly through feelings of guilt and frustration was won around and had spent the preceding day convincing me the idea was sensible. It wasn't that either of us was anxious to kick but rather that conditions we were surrounded by had forced us to seek a means of escape.

We both had obtained our seaman's papers at about the same time but had never made a trip together and in some respects the plan was appealing.

At any rate he was now standing over me insisting I get up so that we could go down to the ship companies for jobs.

Bozo was wandering around the kitchen preparing coffee while making little snide remarks about my general indifference to the more practical aspects of life.

Bob had promptly rolled over pulling the blankets up around his ears and mumbling to the effect he wished we'd get the hell out so he could go back to sleep.

And so I got up.

I had saved a little fix and after getting straight and dressed while Phil and Bozo sat gossiping about what a dear, fine female Kay was and how understanding. After all, there were really few respectable women willing to put up with a junky and at least in Bozo's opinion, Phil should be grateful.

Kay was actually a vampire and eventually drained Phil.

We finally got started and went directly down to a company sending out tankers and were assigned to a ship bound for Honolulu. Phil was signed on as a ship's mess-man and I took utility man in the galley. The man out of the corner of his mouth had told us – "the ship is a hot ship" – meaning that it was scheduled to sail almost immediately – which was good since by this time both of us were anxious to get away as quickly as possible.

We sailed from New Jersey early the following morning. We had rushed around New York all the preceding day, first making a connection – this was to be a slow withdrawal cure – then saying goodbye to acquaintances and friends – making arrangements to have our few possessions taken care of while gone – and a special farewell with Kay. We sailed in a blinding snowstorm.

We had been the last to sign aboard and received what was left of the sleeping quarters. Our fo'c'sle was large enough to accommodate two more – for some reason I never discovered we remained alone – and was situated in the aft end of the ship. It was comfortable and we succeeded in unconsciously turning it into what the captain later suggested looked like an opium den.

Phil immediately climbed into his bunk – staying there for two days, causing the steward to become almost sick with anxiety and to bombard me – though I had provided myself with a good supply of benzedrine and was busy performing my required tasks with what to the steward was amazing vigor – with all sorts of questions. He found it difficult to understand what could possibly be ailing Phil and was somewhat hesitant in accepting my explanation, to the effect he had been drinking – heavily – for the past 98 few weeks. "Don't worry, man, he'll come around. Give him time." To which the steward replied – "I know – but the same can be said for most of the crew – and they're up and working."

The ship was an old ship – having hit the sea about 1915 – and in the rough seas creaked and groaned. It had been making the same run for many years and it wasn't until we entered the Caribbean that it settled down. The trip down the Atlantic Coast was uneventful except that en route we gathered several hundred birds. We would awaken in the morning and there they were, roosting all over the ship, and when we began reaching the area off the Florida coast they began departing. By the time we passed through Windward Passage most of them were gone. I don't know what kind of birds they were – although I did recognize an owl which was almost the last to leave – but I was much impressed by them and they were the first of a series of natural phenomena to fill me with awe and wonder during the voyage.

The crew was an interesting group of old-time seamen – the kind that one sees hanging around the bars on South Street along the waterfront in New York, in the Seamen's Institute, or sitting around in groups, passing a bottle of wine among themselves and looking like typical bums. Not one of them had even been to Maritime School and Kings Point was only a name as far as they were concerned. One old deck hand had been around the world eighteen times and could tell stories about every port he had been in. They were a rugged lot filled with a sense of joy of living I have never encountered in any similar number. They were all friends and many had sailed together for a long period of time.

Phil and I were rather outsiders and it took a while before they accepted us into their confidence. Phil was more successful than I in making friends with them, and when he finally came out of his two-day sleep it was no time until he knew practically everybody.

The captain was an old Dutchman, burly and gruff, who stayed much to himself in his own quarters. The only time I heard him speak was after he received a report from the steward – this happened outside Aruba as we were leaving on our way toward Panama – that I had refused to sort 99 some old rotten potatoes – suggesting that if the steward wanted it done he do it himself – and besides it wasn't my job – and that he didn't know what to do about Phil and me – we were good workers but inclined to do as we pleased. The captain had come to our fo'c'sle and after looking around said – "Goddamn – this looks like an opium den. You guys hopheads?" This was said in a heavy gutteral accent. We both assured him such was not the case and he left telling us – "Try and get along with the steward – who is a damn fool."

We had an exceptionally fine time in Aruba. As a matter of fact the captain was closer to the truth than he knew – since while in Aruba we had picked up on yen-pox and had stayed knocked out the whole time we were there.

Aruba is a small island and very tropical as to climate. We had not been there an hour when out of the clear blue sky a sudden cloud appeared and unleashed a deluge of rain which lasted a short time and then disappeared, leaving once again the blue and gold day. The rain evaporated quickly and everything was left dry.

The people of Aruba are a mixture of light and dark and all very beautiful. There are several nationalities and it was from a Chinese we had obtained the yen-pox.

Phil became involved with a little dark-skinned girl who after they had balled kept trailing him around begging him to stay. We stayed three days.

It was while sailing thru the Caribbean Sea I first became aware of how insignificant I am in comparison to the vastness of the universe.

The sea all day remains a magnificent sparkling surface of blue – deep indigo – undulating in long rolling swells. Schools of spangle-blue flying fish skim the top. Porpoises race and leap in constant play. And at night the sky overhead is either a vast expanse of stars – some of which streak across space in splendid motion which when beheld quickens the heart – or is blanketed with great heavy clouds – black and rolling – lit from above with ceaseless flashing lightning while the sea glitters with balls of tossing phosphorous light. The air is warm and scented with the odor from the distant jungles. One has a sense of concentration
100 of energy and sizzling, crackling electrical force, which seems

to be waiting to tear the universe asunder.

It was on such a night we were steaming steadily toward Colon when Phil and myself, along with two others – one a fellow who shortly after we became acquainted had produced a cigar box full of pot, so that we had been smoking pot for the entire trip thus far – and the other who had eyes for Phil and had been wooing him by stealing morphine styrettes from the life boats, presenting them to him and beseeching him to have a ball – were sitting and lying on the aft end of the ship, watching the wake and exclaiming about the night and laughing and sometimes singing. The gay boy had been pressing Phil to go below with him and making various remarks full of suggestive sexual connotation – finally capping himself when he suddenly exclaimed while observing a large, almost perfectly round puff of black smoke which had been emitted from the ships funnel and was hanging nearly motionless overhead – "Oh, look – it's just like a big dinge nut."

We arrived in Colon and were given immediate shore leave. Phil and I lost no time in searching out the native section and were successful in obtaining cocaine and undoubtedly the finest pot I have ever smoked. The man who helped us make the connection was really a cat. He was tall and very dark skinned, dressed in a delicate pink shirt, light – almost white color – slacks, and a large-brimmed Panama straw hat with a brilliant red band and sandals. He moved with truly feline grace and spoke softly thru shiny white teeth. Phil had left me standing in front of a farmacia – the whole store front open to the street – while he was inside with the proprietor wildly searching the shelves looking for anything remotely resembling junk – and I had become interested in two children who were playing some kind of game when he appeared at my side and said, "Hi, man – my name is Victor – you want to get straight?"

He led me down a street – unpaved and with the houses all sitting back from the walk and wide open so that I could see into them – their occupants and what they were doing. It was a still, hot tropical night and pervading the whole street was the aroma of burning pot. Several young girls with high breasts and tight dresses passed us, giggling and swinging their hips and flashing big smiles at Victor, who 101 pretended not to notice. Kerosene lamps and candles shed the only light except that of the night overhead. The scent of lilies blended with and perfumed the pot smoke. Suddenly Victor halted and said – "Wait here, man" – and disappeared. I stood there in wonder and delight. He returned soon and laid a long package – the length of a sheet torn from a Saturday Evening Post, and big around as a half dollar – of pot in my hands and then said – "You want cocaine – I get." I said yes and once again I was alone. As before he returned quickly. I gave him the money – something like ten or twelve dollars – and returned to where Phil, who had settled for a hypodermic needle and pockets full of nembutal, seconal, ambutal was waiting. We said goodbye to Victor and started back toward the docks to catch the launch to the ship, which lay anchored out in the bay. En route we bought a small white-faced monkey from a boy who had him on a long chain and was teasing him with a stick, causing him to screech and jump.

We kept him in our fo'c'sle where he occupied the section set aside for two other men. I took one of the bunk springs and set it on end facing the bulkhead and he slept on top and would climb up and down the springs. He was comparatively clean, in that he pissed and shit pretty much in one spot and most of the time I newspapers which I spread over in his section. He had the run of the fo'c'sle – and took over. When he was pleased or content or after having been fed something he liked – grapes were his favorite dish – he would chitter and show his teeth, but when annoyed or angry – especially if scolded – would set up a din of screeching which could chill one to the bone.

The trip thru the locks was interesting. We stopped in Balboa for a short time but not long enough for shore leave – and then out into the Pacific Ocean.

Life aboard ship had settled down to a more or less even routine. We were making it on benzedrine – nembutal – seconal – ambutal – a fairly steady supply of morphine styrettes and pot.

Jocko – the monkey – took to pot like the proverbial duck to water, and as soon as I would light up would jump up on my shoulder and I would exhale the smoke into his little grinning face. He and I would get high and he would balance himself on the rail while I leaned up against it and looked at the sea. He would talk to me in little chittering sounds and I would tell him about how cute and great I thought he was. One day we saw a huge fish leap out of the sea and plunge back in again. The sea was a molten gray mass with a veil of shimmering vapor hanging just above the surface – reflecting the burning sun – when suddenly it seemed almost to shatter. This huge fish – glistening in the light – exploded into the air for a moment amidst a spray of crystal drops of water – arched – and slid back into the sea. We were both surprised. Jocko actually screeched and I almost yelled – to him – "did you dig that?"

Phil had decided to augment his finances by playing poker – and at this time spent much of his free time practicing how to stack the deck. I don't remember him being very competent at it but at any rate he didn't lose. The games would occasionally last all night and continued until we reached Honolulu.

We didn't spend enough time in Honolulu for me to absorb much of an impression of it. I recall several bars of nondescript nature where we drank rum – a small amusement part – Dole's Pineapple – palm trees – hundreds of soldiers and sailors – the Y.M.C.A. where I mailed a postcard to somebody – clean streets – high prices – tapa cloth, which I like – and of course the beach and the glass-clear water and its turquoise blue color. Also, we were completely unsuccessful as to pot or junk, although we did make a drugstore for a fresh supply of Benzedrine. I must admit that what little I saw of the islands from the ship was beautiful – and I might like going back sometime. Unfortunately – everything is too Americanized and concerned with the tourists.

We returned by the same route, and just before getting back to Balboa it was time for the full moon – and for several nights I lay up on deck moon-struck. We sailed in a long silver lane. Everything lay revealed in the light of the moon and wore a glowing aura – mysterious to the night – and became new – retaining but little relationship to what it was in the brightness of the sun. Everything was bathed in opalescence. The night became a sort of day – strange and weird as if of another world or planet.

103

Once again we anchored in Balboa. We picked up supplies – bananas, oranges, green stuff, grapes and some staples – and then on back thru the Canal to Colon, where we sailed past while I stood on the deck with Jocko sending telepathic messages to Victor – telling him I would never forget him and that I'd try and make the scene again sometime and to please remember me. We continued on thru the Caribbean, celebrating the New Year with beer and ice cream, and back up past the Florida coast after catching a glimpse of Haiti, and the Atlantic Coast – minus birds – into Chesapeake Bay to Newport News and the end of the voyage.

I left Jocko aboard the ship with one of the crew members who was signing back on and who promised me he would try and set him free – or at least see to it he got a good home, maybe in Aruba or even Colon. I would have liked keeping him, but it would have been cruel of me to bring him here to New York. The weather was exceedingly cold as well, and Jocko belonged in the tropics. I could have smuggled him ashore without any trouble.

Phil and I, after we were paid off, took the train for New York and could hardly wait to make our first connection. Junkwise the trip had been great. Habit-kicking was a complete failure, but neither one of us – as I said before – really wanted to kick.

Bozo was still wandering back and forth between Creedmore – where he had a job as an attendant – and the apartment – bickering and fretting. Bob had gotten himself involved in some big vague scheme and was rushing around in a Benzedrine whirl. Kay could hardly wait to sink her teeth into Phil.

Phil left me in front of the apartment after we had made arrangements for a meet the following day, and I went upstairs – rolled up the last of the fine Panamanian pot, flopped down, and got stoned thinking about Jocko, Victor, the Caribbean Sea and the whole trip.

BILL BURROUGHS

The first year or two of my acquaintance with Bill remained ordinary in the sense of what is usual in the early stages of any friendship between two people. We gradually began to relax – or at least I did – and a degree of respect for one another evolved. I believe Bill found me interesting and someone he could use as a sort of showpiece to exhibit before his more conservative associates – as an example of an underworld type – and someone he could rely upon to be amusing and colorful. My story-telling ability has always stood me in good stead, and even then my experience had been varied and considerably out of the ordinary as far as Bill's friends were concerned. Frankly, I derived a certain pleasure in being candid and open about myself, and nothing pleased me more than an appreciative group of listeners.

Allen was very young at the time and still rather confused about his future and what he wanted or exactly what he would do once school was over. As always he was filled with love and deep-felt desire to communicate with his fellow men. Then as now he was ready to believe in the best in those he met and we became very good friends. Allen has never failed me and has always been quick to offer a helping hand. He held Bill in admiration and has seen only goodness and kindness in him. Frequently we haven't seen eye to eye regarding Bill. Still I firmly believe Allen's awareness of what lies below the surface of Bill's personality has been perhaps closer to the truth than my own. But then Allen sees life with a less jaundiced eye than I.

And then there was Jack Kerouac – who regarded everyone with suspicion but looked up to Bill and dreamed of becoming a writer.

We were a strange group, although there were many others, and along with Joan, we were the people who formed the inner circle. As closely as I am able to recall we were the most constant companions of Bill's life.

Prior to the time I am speaking of, Bill had spent much

of his life in various schools. He had traveled and done much that most people live an entire lifetime without experiencing. He was then and is now one of the most erudite men I've ever known.

Time passed and about two years after making his acquaintance, through a series of unexpected happenings – drug addiction, his and Joan's relationship, departure from New York, and a desire to experiment with the possibilities of growing marijuana and Oriental poppies, maybe manufacturing opium – Joan, her daughter Julie (4 years of age), Bill and myself lived together in Texas. I look back to it as one of my greatest experiences and also as the time I finally learned to understand Bill to a great extent and to at last respect him as I have few people in my life.

Following a general breaking up of the close group – or better a spreading out: with Allen and Kerouac going their respective ways—Allen to sea as a merchant seaman and Jack going into seclusion at home where apparently he continued working at becoming a writer; others drifting homeward to other states and cities – Bill and Joan and Julie began looking for a place somewhere in the Southwest they could settle in a while, and finally located the beautiful little cabin we lived in through the last of the winter of 1946 and up until September or almost October of 1947. It was situated on the edge of a piece of property consisting of some 97 acres in the midst of a pine woods which began at the top of a gentle incline – with the cabin there in an enclosed yard or fenced-in area at the top and several sheds and an old collapsing barn – and then rolled downward to a bayou, twisting and turning its way through the country – a place of heavy tropical vines and spanish-moss-draped trees – where sunlight filtered through the heavy lush green-growing vegetation and one felt one could get lost – or have strange adventures – and that it had always been there since the beginning of time – and had barely felt the intrusion of man. It was wild and beautiful and mysterious, and I always imagined I was entering a great steaming jungle each time I would go down to explore its shadowed depths.

The preceding year had been hectic and discouraging for me and I was extremely anxious to depart New York. All through the month of December and immediately following the first of the year I had spent much time following up the possibility of obtaining a berth aboard a tanker and of going back to sea. I had been given a lead on a tanker company that had sold a number of their ships to the Chinese and were supposedly anxious to sail their ships to Shanghai where the crew was to be discharged, given plane tickets back to the States and then rehired in order to staff another ship bound for China to once again follow the same procedure of disembarking – flying back to the States and once again making the same voyage – or to perhaps become a member of a crew sailing elsewhere. It sounded made to order for me, and the afternoon I received word from Bill and Joan – plus fare and expenses for joining them in Texas – I had been given notice to report the following day at one of the piers in Brooklyn, to board a ship ready for sailing to Shanghai. I had been hired as a second cook at a salary of $350 per month – with an additional bonus of $500 payable upon my return to New York. I am unable to recall what the bonus was supposedly for or what risk or inconvenience it justified but it sounded attractive – and besides just the mere thought of leaving N.Y.C. was stimulating. One can easily see my dilemma when Joan and Bill's message arrived and it became my problem to immediately reach a decision of whether it be Texas with Joan and Bill or China and a quick return to N.Y.C. plus a good supply of money, and that had long been a desperate need. Let it suffice that my curiousity and love for Joan tiped the scale in favor of joining Burroughs and helping him with his plans for experimenting with the soilless growth of marijuana and Oriental poppies. The idea was, if successful, I might become his partner in developing an American opium outlet and perhaps corner a small part of the already thriving and fantastically lucrative junk business. I immediately wired Texas announcing my date and hour of arrival.

In the most recent of Joan's letters she had spoken of the remoteness of their location and therefore when they sent my ticket it was for as far as Houston where I would be met by Bill and driven in his jeep by him the last fifty miles to the little town of New Waverly which was exactly 12 miles from where Bill had settled and was the nearest town or community of any size to his place.

Until then my dealings with Bill had been mostly brief and usually of a business nature. He had been much more closely involved with Phil White. He had met Phil the same night he met me about two years previously. We met a very short time after my return from a great trip along with Phil down through the Caribbean Sea, the Panama Canal and into the Pacific to Hawaii and back. Phil and myself became crew members of this old tanker just at the end of the war, and although we had not been overly anxious to make any trip at the time, we were nonetheless rather concerned with cutting down our narcotic habits and this trip seemed ready-made for the purpose when we first set sail. It worked out quite the opposite, and although the voyage had been great and exciting it thoroughly failed to fulfill the original purpose. We returned still hooked and perhaps using a shade less junk than at the beginning. Running directly into an old queen and acquaintance who had access to the ship's medical supplies – plus no compunction about stealing the morphine Syrettes from the lifeboat kits – had been the major cause of our continued use of stuff, even while at sea. There was something ludicrous about going to sea ostensibly to stop using junk and completely failing. Just who in hell expects to board a ship out from the mainland and then discover shortly after losing sight of the shore that they have just run into the proverbial one chance in a thousand, the one person – the medical officer excluded – who has a direct line to the medical supplies and, at the same time, immediately becomes enamored with one's partner and friend, and is more than willing to turn over the keys of the ship's stores or do anything at all within his scope to prove his love and willingness to cooperate toward making his loved one happy?

Both Phil and myself had squandered our payoff quickly – it was comparatively small. Both of us had spent a great deal of money in each of the ports we stopped in and had drawn heavily on our salaries. About a week and a half after our return we were sitting talking in the pad we were staying in on Henry Street (Bill describes the place fairly accurately in his first book – "Junkie") and waiting for Bob

Brandenburg to get home. Bob was a young cat who worked up near Columbia University as a soda jerk and shared the pad with us. We expected to borrow enough money from him to pay for the filling of the prescription for morphine we had gotten from one of the Brooklyn doctors we were seeing at the time. We had used our last money to pay the doctor and so far we had met nothing but refusal and apologetic explanation from everyone we'd asked to borrow from and so Bob was our last hope. Neither Phil nor I was sure of what we'd do if Bob failed us, and therefore we were in rather depressed moods when Bob finally arrived bringing Bill Burroughs – Wm. S. Burroughs, and later alias Bull Lee – with him.

Bozo, who owned the apartment, was cleaning and washing after dinner in the kitchen. Phil and I were sitting talking at the kitchen table and gossiping with Bozo.

Bob introduced Bill and we asked him to join us at the table. He looked around as he was taking his coat off and finally, handing both his hat and coat to Bob, sat down. Bob had gone on through to the bedroom and was preparing to settle down for the evening, busily moving about from one room to another, constantly talking and asking questions. Phil and Bill were becoming acquainted and Bozo was offering everyone tea or coffee and half apologizing because of his surroundings and the general slum nature of the neighborhood. I had observed Bill only a moment or two but decided I didn't feel friendly toward him – sizing him up in my mind as dull-appearing and a bit smug and self-opinionated and certainly not very hip. Looking at him intently it entered my mind he could conceivably be a policeman or plainclothesman – maybe even F.B.I. – he looks cold-blooded enough to be one. That old Chesterfield coat he's wearing went out of style fifteen years ago, and that snap-brim hat: Don't he think he's the rogue. Those glasses – he looks as conservative as they come in them. Glasses without rims must make him feel like he's not wearing glasses at all. I don't like him and if Bob doesn't ask him to leave, I will. I finally stepped into the other room with Bob – speaking to him of my suspicions and asking him where and how he had met Bill, and most of all why he had brought him home. Bob laughed and reassured me. Bill was trying to pick up a 109 little easy money by selling a hot sawed-off machine gun. Bob explained he had become acquainted with Bill at the soda fountain of the drugstore where he worked. He said Bill aparently was a steady customer – usually shopping in the store some time during each afternoon and then stopping at the fountain for a soft drink and a chat. They had become friendly and one afternoon Bill had asked Bob if he had any idea of where he might sell the gun. Bob had been delighted with the question, undoubtedly flattered because of Bill's confidence. Bob wanted nothing quite so much as recognition as an underworld character – preferably in the nature of being thought of in terms of racketeer-gangster and all around hipster. Bob had spoken of Phil and myself and of the scene in general at the apartment and had asked Bill to await our return and then Bob would escort him downtown and in all probability either Phil or I – or perhaps he himself – would be able to negotiate some kind of deal.

I wasn't completely convinced of Bill's harmlessness and used several arguments in favor of having Bill depart and had almost reached the point of taking the matter into my own hands when suddenly I heard Phil say – "What's that you just said, Bill? You have morphine? What are they – morphine Syrettes? That sounds very interesting. How many?" Bill and Phil had been hitting it off splendidly and the one thing needed to solidify Phil's interest in his behalf was the mention of having drugs in his possession. Already Bill was telling him of how a friend had come into possession of a least a gross of morphine Syrettes and had given them to him to dispose of. He continued, saying, "I am not sure but I think there was a holdup in a drugstore and one of the stick-up men was his friend and had decided after cleaning out the cash-register to investigate the narcotics cabinet and seeing this huge package marked morphine – without thinking twice he grabbed it. Later he came to me and asked me to see if I could get rid of them at a profit. Also he gave me this goddamned machine gun. I don't want the damned thing and want to sell it."

Phil had listened closely and as Bill finished his little speech Phil called to me, saying – "Hey, Huncke, our friend here has some morphine. He says he wants to sell the stuff and will let it go cheaply." Bill interrupted to say, "Well – as a matter of fact I want to sell all but one or two of these Syrettes. The one or two I keep I'd like to try taking – in order to see what the experience of taking an addictive drug is like. Have either of you any knowledge of this stuff, and if so do you know how it is taken?"

Phil began laughing and I found myself amused, since we had been using exactly what Bill had to offer and instinctively I knew Phil was already scheming some way to latch onto the supply and for as little financial outlay as possible. I knew my desire to lay hold of the stuff was actively developed, and although I still didn't feel that Bill should be trusted, in thinking about it I couldn't see where Phil and myself could get into too much trouble since it was Bill who was trying to make some money on the deal – and deciding to sound out Phil concerning his feelings in the matter, I abruptly departed from Bob and joined Bill and Phil at the kitchen table. Phil needed no prodding and had started to discuss price and the matter of showing Bill how to take off. Bill had brought a few of the Syrettes with him and no no time we three – Bill, Phil and I – were in the process of shooting up.

Bill was by this time obviously enjoying himself and I had to admit to myself just possibly he was a nice person trying to experience something a bit more exciting than what he was usually involved with, and he was apparently honest about his interest in drugs.

In attempting to recall the whole scene I find I am unable to do so completely. I can't remember how the gun was finally disposed of – or if it was, for that matter – nor exactly what arrangements were made about the rest of the morphine. Let it suffice Bill took an immediate liking for taking drugs, and soon he and Phil were animatedly discussing the use of stuff – the various forms of drugs – how long Phil had been using – how long I had used – of our serving time for possession – how miserable it was kicking – and everything else either of them could think of in the way of questions and answers.

Bill and Phil arranged to keep in touch with each other and shortly after coming to terms regarding Phil and myself buying the Syrettes, Bill departed.

It was the beginning of a whole new life for Bill. At that 111 time I saw very little of either of them and was a bit surprised about one week later to run into the two of them about 1:30 in the morning getting ready to take the subway at 72nd Street and Broadway. Just what it was that had caused me to be that far uptown at the time I don't recall, but I can remember wondering a bit what the two had in common. They informed me they were making the hole together as partners, with Bill learning to act as a shill and cover-up man for Phil – helping him to pick pockets by standing near, holding a newspaper open, spread wide – Phil reaching behind Bill, fingers feeling the inside breast pocket of the mark's suit jacket or perhaps the overcoat pockets searching for the wallet – or poke, as Phil referred to it. Somehow there was something ludicrous about a man of Bill's obvious educational background becoming a business partner with knock-around, knock-down, hard-hustling Phil, who had forgotten more about scuffling for money illegally than most people ever learn. Still, dope or junk has created many a strange relationship, and this was certainly no more unusual than many I'd run across. My feelings were it would undoubtedly be a great experience for Bill, and also I was glad Phil seemed to be doing fairly well – and I guessed Bill was at least indirectly responsible for Phil's seeming good luck. The three of us talked together a short while and I learned they had been in constant touch since the evening of their first meeting, and that already Bill had a habit – not a very big habit, but a habit nonetheless – and that they had been making doctors for scripts. The Syrettes had long been used up and Phil had immediately coached Bill on how to make a doctor. According to Phil, Bill had been a natural. Just before saying goodbye, we all three decided to meet the following day and I would join them on their forage for scripts. Phil had spoken of several doctors he could no longer make but that he felt sure I could. He mentioned their names to Bill and he agreed it was more than likely. Also three people making doctors would in the end be able to obtain considerably more stuff than just two people. And so we soon began learning a little about Bill and his life.

My life at the time was in the usual state of chaos with three- and four-day periods of no sleep – making it in a

Benzedrine haze – hallucinating – walking along the edge of Central Park peering intently into each clump of bushes, the shadows alive with strange shapes and formations – or of sitting many hours at a stretch in some cafeteria talking with the people of my acquaintance who made up the majority of the Times Square population – a varied and rootless group, frequently homeless and alone, existing from day to day, lonely and oddly frightened, but invariably alert and full of humor and always ready for the big chance – the one break sure to earn them security and realization of the ever-present dream.

Often toward the early dawn hours Bill, Phil and myself would wind up our night consuming cup after cup of coffee – well into the day, so late we were rather early morning – ready to visit our various doctors and pick up as many prescriptions for morphine or dilaudid as possible. We all three grumbled and complained, swearing we would prefer almost any other method for keeping ourselves straight. Yet in retrospect it was somehow stimulating and cause for amusement – at least conversationally – particularly when Bill would bait Phil about some episode involving one his doctor's wives who had someway learned of her husband's enterprising nature and his illegal manner of increasing his income, and had decided to take matters into her own hands. She had started by refusing to allow Phil to see the doctor, using a flimsy excuse and lecturing Phil about vice and corruption and finally backing out of Phil's way when he had barked some foul oath or other at her – telling her to shut the fuck up, that he intended seeing her husband whether she allowed it or not. Bill had found Phil's description of the scene extremely humorous and enjoyed getting Phil wound up.

About then Bill had discovered a small apartment on the same street Bozo's place was, and as the rent was cheap he rented it, presumably intending to move in and set up a sort of studio and working quarters for himself. He was always rather vague about exactly what sort of work he wished to do, and it was some time later I learned of his wish to write.

At the time Bill rented his apartment downtown I was spending most of my time on and around 42nd Street, 113 hustling, stealing and simply hanging around – frequenting several of the bars and cafeterias either on 42nd Street or somewhere else in the Times Square area. It was my third of fourth year on the scene and not only was I well known, but I had become a figure or character in my own right and very little transpired within the immediate vicinity I wasn't aware of. It was about then Kinsey began his investigation or survey of the sex habits of Americans. He had come to New York and intended interviewing as many people as possible, starting with the colleges and finally arriving at Times Square. I was one of the first people he made contact with, and after our interview he suggested my recommending him to as many of my acquaintances as possible. This I was more than willing to do, and in no time we had established a sort of business friendship. I spent much of my time hanging out in a bar on 8th Avenue and 43rd Street, and quite often he would stop by and invite me to have dinner with him. One evening Bill joined us and thereafter it was not unusual for Bill, Kinsey and many of Bill's friends and myself to sit in a booth talking, so that we formed a kind of group of seemingly good friends – and although I remained somewhat skeptical of Bill, it was during the time of these gatherings I began to feel friendlier towards him and to respect him.

PART II

Bill moved uptown near Columbia to an apartment owned by Joan Adams. She was studying at Columbia. She was in all probability one of the most charming and intelligent women I've ever met. She and Bill were immediately attracted to each other and from then until her death several years later she and Bill were never separated for very long. She loved Bill ardently and I am quite sure worshiped him in a manner most women seldom attain. He shot her accidentally causing her death.

I of course was an outsider to his environment at the time they met and when one evening after he and I had been talking and drinking coffee in Bickford's 42nd Street cafeteria he invited me to visit him uptown and meet his friends, it didn't enter my mind for a moment I would soon be one of the members of his immediate crowd or that from then on our lives would become permanently linked. Yet that is exactly what happened and even now – although we have drifted apart – there is still a very positive bond between us. It was through Bill I met Allen, who, in a very strange way, had had more influence on my life than anyone else I've known.

When I began seeing Bill and his friends constantly – that is, every day, practically living with them, learning to know them more intimately in a way than I had known my own family – my feelings concerning almost all of them, with perhaps one exception—Joan—were those of indifference and to some degree hostility. They were all so very, very intellectual – I felt as though at best they were patronizing toward me, and that there was no real feeling of warmth or affection from any of them. Still, they were at the very least interesting, and in a sense – against my will – I found myself becoming involved with them to such an extent it became impossible for me to imagine pulling away. Finally when I was arrested and served my time and returned to find them still friendly and concerned, the die was cast. Since then we have all remained closely connected.

At the time of my arrest Bill was indirectly involved and his family felt it would be an excellent idea for him to leave New York. Following his family's wishes, he and Joan set out for Texas, where they remained for a little longer than a year and where I joined them for a good part of that time.

As I have already mentioned I corresponded with Joan and Bill and upon receipt of their invitation to join them in Texas I immediately accepted.

I met Bill in Houston and we began our drive out to the cabin. Bill was looking well and seemed enthusiastic about his plans. He told me he had been using a little paregoric and pantapon which Bill Garver sent him fairly regularly through the mail. He said Joan was using Benzedrine and that he was running into difficulty keeping up the supply. He said he had made every town within a radius of fifty miles three or four times already, and he was afraid people were beginning to wonder a little about just what was going on. He said things were in pretty bad shape at the house, and a great deal of work had to be done to make the place livable. He explained that he and Joan were staying at a motel and had been going out to the cabin every day trying to shape things up. He said the bad weather would break soon and then the place would be easier to reach.

He had located in east Texas and we drove fifty miles from Houston over paved highways to the town of New Waverly—a small-sized town about five blocks long, a few stores and a filling station—just off the main highway. We drove on through New Waverly and onto a black macadam road which began turning and twisting as soon as we left the town and continued the same all the way to where we turned off onto a sand and gravel road into the pine woods. We had covered 12 miles from New Waverly through countryside sparsely dotted with small farms and occasional houses alongside the road. It was beautiful country and as we drove Bill commented about the people and of the probably near arrival of spring. We finally reached the beginning of the woods on either side and then the turn-off. The weather was grey and damp and Bill had said maybe it would be necessary to park the jeep and walk the last half mile because he was afraid of getting stuck. We remained on the dirt road which had made a little dip. We drove down one side of the dip and just before driving up the opposite side we crossed an old wooden plank bridge. The pine woods were thick on either side and I couldn't help but wonder just what they hid from view. Every so often there would be a rural mailbox and a road way off leading off the road, but there was no other evidence of people or their houses. We remained on the gravel and dirt road about two miles and as we came to a pair of car tracks which led into the woods Bill slowed down and turned the jeep onto them. We drove a short distance into the woods and I could have touched the trees alongside without difficulty. Suddenly Bill stopped the jeep. He said we had better walk the rest of the way.

My first impression of the entire scene was that we had found a sort of paradise, and I never changed my feelings. It was a truly beautiful section. The cabin was weather-worn—silver grey—and it appeared to have grown out of the earth instead of having been constructed. It was sturdy and comfortable, and by the time we were finished repairing and straightening everything out it was a snug little place.

Time flew and spring burst all around us. Then came summer and the heat. And before any of us really realized it, fall was upon us – our crops were picked and we were ready to split back to New York.

Talking or speaking of all that took place during that period of time would fill many pages. Let it suffice – it was an experience I'll perhaps never forget. Bill's son was born in July and by the time we were ready to leave Bill had been a father of almost three months' standing.

Bill had thoroughly enjoyed himself. He had played the role of the country squire. He had guns – he even acquired a small hound pup before we left. One thing worth mentioning I think is the first time – the occasion on which – I saw him in a completely new way. It happened one weekend in Houston and I realized for the first time that he was a handsome man.

I spent many weekends in Houston. I had discovered a drugstore where I was able to purchase as many Benzedrine inhalers and all the barbiturates I wished – and paregoric in half gallons, if I so desired – and therefore when I'd hit

Houston it would be for the purpose of picking up supplies. I'd usually take the bus from New Waverly and return the following night about 11:30, and Bill would meet me and we'd drive back to the cabin.

On the weekend I referred to I had several things to do besides pick up drug supplies, and Bill had half-heartedly mentioned the possibility of his falling into Houston some time Saturday afternoon. I had hit Houston late Friday and wasn't planning to return until Sunday evening. As soon as I'd arrived in Houston I'd go directly to the Brayos Hotel, which was located alongside Houston's Chinatown. It had been a good hotel at one time, and still gave good service although it was somewhat removed from the main section of downtown. I had checked in late and all they had left was a two-room suite, which I took. It was late in June and the weather was intensely hot.

I had made friends with several colored cats in the colored section downtown where I'd cop some pot, and one of the cats who owned a record store would let me borrow one of his record players – and I'd hook it up in my room and turn on while listening to some good sound which my man had either recommended or I had selected.

This weekend had been no different – except when I hit the hotel after picking up the record player I ran into a cat who was a seaman – young, maybe twenty or twenty-one – and after talking with him a while invited him up to my rooms. He was a beautiful cat and he spent the night with me – smoking and talking and listening to records. He had never actually relaxed and listened to jazz before, and he was very impressed with what he heard. We had enjoyed ourselves and were both a little surprised when there was a knock on the door. And when I asked who was there, Bill replied. I let him in and after introducing him to my friend asked him if he was planning to stay overnight and take me back with him the next day. He replied that he wasn't sure, but that he had simply wanted to get away from the scene at the cabin and come to Houston. As well as getting reading material and a fresh supply of liquor, he wanted very much to take a bath.

While he had been telling me this the phone rang, and when I answered it was my pot man – and I arranged to meet him. Meanwhile Bill had seated himself and was busy talking with my friend. I excused myself – explaining I had to keep a meet with the pot man – and after observing the two of them a few minutes to see if they would get along, I split out.

I kept my meet, copped, and sat around talking with the connection and his old lady a little while and smoked a couple of joints. I was away about two hours, and when I returned – not only had they both gotten along, but the two of them were stone cold drunk.

I had seen Bill slightly intoxicated many times, but this was the first time I'd seen him really drunk. When I came in Bill was sitting – straddling a straight-back chair – apparently deeply engrossed in whatever he had been discussing with my friend, who sat facing him in an armchair. Both of them were half-crocked, drunken leers on their faces. They greeted me with real cheery hellos and assured me I should join them in having a drink. Bill reached over toward an almost empty bottle of tequila and said – "Come on, Huncke, have a little snort. It'll make you feel great." He fumbled around looking for his glass and said I could drink from the glass he'd been drinking from. I thanked him and refused, telling him I thought he had had enough also, and wondering what I was going to do about him. It was obvious he could barely sit up, much less stand.

"Bill, come on – no more please. I think maybe you better stretch out on the bed."

He stood up and rocked back and forth a couple of times and then made straight for the bed and half fell onto it in a big heap. I walked over and helped him stretch out. I removed his glasses, which had fallen askew across his face. He was half laughing and mumbling something I couldn't understand. It was at that moment – as he closed his eyes and then opened them again – looking around, then giving a big sigh – closed them and fell into a deep sleep almost instantly – as I watched him, I began to see his face in a manner I hadn't seen it before – and I was startled as I recognized the beauty of his features – his coloring and his whole being – relaxed and graceful on the bed. His hair had fallen down over one side of his forehead like a cowlick, and he looked like a strange other-world creature. His eyelids 119 were tinged faintly lavender and belonged with the sharp aquiline nose and the well-shaped mouth now almost closed the lips red and finely drawn – the corners of his mouth smooth and free of tense lines. He was certainly handsome and although his entire coloring was delicate and there was nothing harshly masculine in his appearance, there was nothing feminine either. His was a man's face.

I was very touched, and at that instant a certain feeling of love I bear for him to this day sprang into being. I had always known him quick with verbal explanation and always logical and practical. He had always seemed complete master of himself, and now – seeing him defenseless and vulnerable – I understood he was lonely and in many ways as bewildered as anyone else.

I have never forgotten those few moments, and recently when I saw him – an older, more self-contained and seemingly satisfied man – every now and then while we talked, the other Bill would come through much the same as then.

We left Texas finally and drove back to New York. We did some business together with the pot but we began seeing less of each other. Things had changed considerably for everyone. Allen was beginning to take on stature and was doing a lot of writing. Jack had his first book almost completed and Phil had disappeared somewhere with his old lady. New York was different also. The Times Square scene was undergoing rapid change. There was a drive on to clean things up and it was being taken seriously. Most of the old haunts were closed and all-night cafeterias were no longer all-night places. I moved away entirely from the midtown area. Bill and Joan were no longer around Manhattan, having settled in Far Rockaway or some such place. Occasionally we'd meet, but Bill was making plans to return toward the southwest – New Orleans this time – and then Mexico.

And so it went. That year came to a close and the next few whipped by. Allen began growing up and Jack was ready for the next big break. My life didn't change too radically, but circumstances kept us all more or less separated. I began seeing Allen more often and soon a sort of pattern was established which remains to this day. Allen 120 has always and still does keep me informed concerning Bill.

The first time I ran into him – about five years after our return from Texas – at first he seemed almost the same. Then, after being in his presence a short while, I recognized an almost imperceptible difference. He seemed more impersonal, with a slight show of interest that was slightly clinical as though one were being observed through a magnifying lens. At first when we met there was an element of snobbishness both intellectually and socially in his dealings with others, and I think even at this point I am speaking of it remained – but he had acquired the habit of not showing it openly – covering it beneath a sort of conversational adroitness. He was pleased to renew our friendship, but underneath or inside I don't believe it touched him very deeply.

Joan was dead and his changes had been many and varied – and I guessed at the time he felt his loneliness intensely, and much of his time was occupied attempting to forget at least most of those happenings which might have helped recall her to mind. Their relationship, from what I personally knew, had been of an extremely intimate nature insofar as Joan was concerned, at least. I am quite firmly convinced she barely recognized the existence of others, with – of course – the exception of her children, whom she loved with pride and great tenderness and understanding. She and Bill had had something rare and certainly, from the standpoint of the observer, very fine and beautiful. Unquestionably the adjustments required of Bill to continue seeking meaning and purpose must have placed him under exhausting strain, and I couldn't help but wonder at his self-control.

We saw each other only briefly – about three or four times – and then he departed for South America. From then on until the present we have seen very little of each other, and the little information I have concerning his private life has reached me by way of Allen.

When he first arrived back in the States after his long sojourn abroad we met several times for dinner and conversation with the idea of renewing our friendship. I had felt reluctant about meeting him, wondering if perhaps his only reason for seeing me was due to some idea he might have concerning a sense of obligation to someone from the past who was still seeing mutual friends but had long ago ceased to mean anything in his life. And then of course there was 121 always curiousity as a possible factor. It appeared almost absurd in my mind that he might genuinely be interested in renewing our friendship – and for that matter I am not completely convinced his original association with me was entirely of a friendly nature, although surely there was no enmity involved. At any rate I couldn't help considering myself rather presumptuous – thinking of the famous William Burroughs in the same breath with good old Bill or Bull or even Bill Burroughs. Still, somewhere back along the line he had touched my heart and besides my curiosity and desire to make comparison of present and past personality differences – if any – demanded I see him at least once regardless of his reasons for seeing me.

He invited me to have dinner with him and I accepted. It was truly enjoyable and doubly so because I came away believing he was honestly glad to see me.

We spoke briefly of his stay in Tangiers and of his writing and of his son. He was amusing concerning Bill Jr. – sounding very much the typical father – berating the youth of today and their seeming indifference to the more important aspects of everyday living, their lack of a sense of responsibility, and his son Bill in particular, who – according to his father's opinion – is incredibly indifferent. At one point in the conversation he said – "Why he didn't even show an interest in the language. Seemed to prefer hanging around bars."

IRVING, IN PART

I met Irving after getting in touch with Allen again after a lapse of about five years. He had been surprised at my re-appearance in his life but was seemingly pleased to see me. He and Peter were living on 2nd Street in the Lower East Side area. Locating him at all presented a problem. I knew he had given poetry readings in several of the coffee houses in the city, but at the time I was unacquainted with their names and locations with the exception of the Gaslight on Macdougal Street, and went there seeking information concerning where I might locate him. The people I first spoke to gave me vague answers, but suggested I remain a while on the slim chance he or one of his friends might come in. I had been there only a short time when Ray and Bonnie Bremser came in. I of course had never seen either of them before, but became aware of them while they were speaking with one of the people I had spoken to – and as they frequently glanced my way during the discussion, I was not in the least surprised when they came over and introduced themselves and asked me why I wanted to find Allen. Ray did most of the talking and when I told him my name he immediately recognized it, telling me he was sure Allen would be glad to see me. He then introduced me to his wife, Bonnie, and suggested we leave. We took a cab directly to Allen's. Ray had some pot and we all turned on while Allen filled me in with details of what had been happening with himself and Jack and Bill and the scene in general. I was impressed and anxious to get around a little and meet a few of his friends. Ray and Bonnie had to leave and Allen suggested he, Peter and myself go out and visit a few spots he was sure I would like, and meet some of the people. We went to a coffee house called the Seven Arts and then to a bar called the Cedar. We met friends and acquaintances of Allen's and Peter's everywhere, and when we started back toward Allen's Allen spoke to Peter and said, "I think Huncke should meet Irving." Peter smiled rather mysteriously and replied – "So 123 do I." Irving lived on 8th Street near Avenue D, and because I knew nothing about the area it seemed we were a very long time getting there – and also I was thoroughly confused about directions – streets – avenues – and the whole district. We climbed five flights of stairs to be admitted by Irving into his apartment.

When I first looked at him I was struck by his coloring. His hair almost black – his eyes deep, deep brown – his complexion ivory-toned, and his lips very red. He was wearing a beard and his hair was long. From our first meeting on I never grew tired of observing his appearance. He is of small stature – his body proportionately constructed on the same scale. His eyes – expressive and always searching – can grow cold and hostile one instant and speculative the next. His features are symmetrical and inclined to be a bit sharp. His mouth is framed with rather thin, well-shaped lips, and when he smiles he shows good white teeth. His movements are gentle and graceful and I will always see him as a little Persian prince.

He was very charming and his enthusiasm about the whole scene appeared genuine. We spoke occasionally while Allen and Peter were busy with a discussion about poetry and poets. Irving asked several fairly direct questions about me, but in such a way I was rather flattered by his interest and enjoyed answering him as honestly as I could. We did not remain long and as we were leaving Irving told me to come back soon.

I can't remember how long it was before I went back to see him but when I did it began a period when I was seeing him frequently – and we became something of a friend to each other. He is an excellent talker and obviously well-schooled and erudite. Enjoyable to be with when in good form.

When we first became friends I discovered he stayed in bed for long periods of time. Also he would not eat. He was very poor and forced to live frugally. He was bitter and depressed. His sense of humor is keen, and I would tell of something I had seen or perhaps of an experience, and I think once in a while my presence was good for him because he would laugh, saying – "Huncke – you have had and do have the most incredible things happen to you."

At first I thought he was defenseless – delicate, and easily taken advantage of – and was rather angry when I heard someone we all knew to be somewhat unscrupulous had been staying with Irving. None of us should have been in the least worried. Irving is strong and has a sense of determination he can call upon in a minute, and will act accordingly. Also, he has a code of moral evaluations he will use to intimidate one if possible, and he is quite positive concerning right and wrong. Irving needs little if any protection – on the contrary, it is those he moves against who require protection. He is crafty and sly and quick. I have seen him dart his hand out in a flash and, with his fingers extended in claw fashion, pick a live mouse off his table – where he had permitted it to get, having watched it, searching for food, finally reach the table top – and calmly walk to the window and drop the live mouse to a smashed death. All this with a smile, the calculated edges of a leer at the corners of his mouth.

I have heard him—when annoyed with someone's behavior—sever connection with that person coldly, and with malice betray the weakness revealed for him alone in gay, not-quite Oscar Wildean drawing-room wit, but with rather a bit more vitriolic deadly intent. He can be extremely kind and considerate as well, and I was firmly convinced I at least could anticipate his reactions and he would never surprise me. I had never for a moment since we became friends felt it would be wise to watch myself with him, and therefore talked as openly to him as I ever have to anyone. He led me to believe he was somewhat captivated by my stories, and when we were alone together he was adept at asking questions aimed at causing me to start talking. We were comfortable together and could and did gossip together with great glee. He was constantly meeting new and beautiful people. There were always people knocking on his door – who came in to stay a while or, as in several instances, to stay indefinitely – and if they only stayed a while and I was still there when they departed, I was sure I would get a little biographical sketch of the person – with little personal embellishments delivered as asides, always very acid but funny. He has always done this with everyone, and I believe he is almost at his best at these times.

Irving is keenly aware of being alone and is unhappy much of the time. Clouds of depression hang heavy around him and he becomes moody and rejects people. His dignity will not allow him to relax, and because of a very basic personal consciousness of fastidiousness about manners and conduct and good and evil it is impossible for him to trust anyone beyond a certain point. He is firmly convinced he is being hustled – taken advantage of – or being used, and when aroused feels a need to pass judgement – deciding on the instant to act decisively and in defense of his level of perception. He will without hesitation destroy your most precious possession of the moment, blandly announcing his action is motivated by only what he has decided is to be for your own good.

I had never seen him really let go, nor thought I would ever be the one his finger would point toward in accusation.

I had managed with financial assistance to breathe a little life into the scene – had an O.Z. of good amphets, to use and sell enough of to make up the cost and possibly even realize a little profit.

Irving became a little more excited each time we met, because he thought per chance I would walk away from the Sixth Street pad and arrive at his door some early morning in a state near collapse – my mind a sink-pool of corruption and my brain boiled in amphetamine. I had foolishly developed the habit of visiting him at least once a day, and even now and then twice in one day, giving him minutely detailed accounts of the happenings in and around the Sixth Street apartment. I let myself go completely and failed to realize I was shocking him with my lurid descriptions of Janine's and Bill Heinie's actions toward each other, or of the unending activity and the continual flow of people in and out of the place. He was sure we were all doomed.

On the day of my good fortune with the purchase of the ounce of amphetamine I felt it would be more practical to take it to Irving's – where I knew it would be safe while I made contact with a few of the people I knew were anxious to cop. Elise was staying at Irving's, and on that particular day Ed Marshall had chosen to pay him a visit. Elise opened the door when I knocked and there was Ed. I was an admirer of Elise and spent hour after hour talking with and to her. I felt I had at last succeeded in reaching her, and she was able to grasp my points with knowledge of what I had explained being as close to basic truth at least as far as ourselves and the others of the scene we made contact with were concerned. She liked me and allowed herself to be as open as possible in the circumstances, and suddenly caught the meaning of all I had been talking about since before she decided on moving away from the building in which Allen and Peter were living – and we had thoroughly enjoyed exchanging comments about everything in general on our last two encounters.

Ed had a first-hand experience with the interior of our place on Sixth Street several times in a row, and although it had been exciting and maybe frightening – by his own words – there was no evil and he could hardly go back on his word. In fact, it was always the evil outside which caused the trouble – when dire predictions were forecast and hepatitis sure to develop had you so much as smoked a stick of pot in the place – and if you had been rash enough to use any of the works or amphetamine, you had better rush to a doctor – he might rescue you before it was too late.

These were the conclusions of all the people who had never set foot in the place but had heard the music from down below on the street – and observed the starry-eyed dreamers and creators, thin and haunted-looking, coming and going.

Elise asked me if I had any horse and Ed said he would like just a small taste of the amphets. It so happened I could accommodate them both and we all three took off. I told them of my ounce, asking them to watch out for it while I cut down the street to locate a couple of buyers. I hadn't paid close attention to whether or not Irving was home, but was not surprised when I was about to leave for downstairs I looked up and saw him coming out of his bedroom. We greeted one another pleasantly enough and I said I would be back soon. Irving said nothing, and I walked out in good form because I knew I was going to make some money—badly needed—immediately, and would probably set up a fairly steady operation I could rely on to keep me in 127 money and help me retain independence. It would surely be great to be able to iron out a few hang-ups on Sixth Street caused mainly by lack of money. Also having money would help me apply a little pressure when needed.

I rushed around and ran into Macalee—who was anxious to cop and had ten dollars. We walked back together to Irving's building where Macalee decided to wait below while I went up to make a ten-dollar bag or deck I would bring down to him. I climbed the stairs and knocked, saying my name through the door. Elise let me in, and as I passed her going through the doorway I thought she was looking at me strangely. Ed was standing on one side of the room and Irving walked into the front room and on through to his bedroom. I could not believe I had anything in way of a reprimand coming, and was astonished there was anyone who apparently felt the opposite.

Looking at Ed and Elise I asked them for the amphetamine, saying, "Macalee is downstairs and wants a ten-dollar bag." Elise turned away from me and Ed hung his head, not looking at me, saying at the same time "Huncke I'm sorry. We don't have it any more. After you left Irving demanded we give it to him and when we did, he flushed it down the toilet."

For a moment I was completely stymied. Thoughts began churning around in my mind. It was gone and not even paid for. What was I going to do now. All my hopes for freeing myself of the immediate problem of money, wiped away. It was unbelievable. Why would Irving do such a thing? If he objected to my having the stuff in his house, why hadn't he said so earlier. I hadn't made a secret of it being in my possession. I simply couldn't think straight.

Irving was standing watching me with an almost malevolent expression on his face. He was smirking and quite obviously enjoying my confusion.

Anger surged through me and just what kept me from beating him I'll never know. I did give vent to a verbal onslaught, shouting and yelling at him which did very little to change the situation. Finally still in a rage I slammed out of his apartment threatening to never speak to him again. But of course, eventually I did speak to him again.

I am sure it doesn't matter one way or another but I

have never truly liked him since then and at this point, hope I will never find it necessary to be in his company again.

THE PARTY

Friday evening last week began a strange course of events. It in all probability was a culmination point. The entire day carried an aura of the unusual, and as evening began—late afternoon, about 5 o'clock—returning from an errand where I work I walked in on Janine, sitting doing calligraphy—her legs crossed, head bent low, a huge carpetbag by her side. She was wearing heels – silken stockings – a very pale blue and light beige colored frock – designed to fit tightly thru the bodice – a round low neckline – semi-puffed sleeves – short – exposing the leg to about the knees. She owns a dilapidated straw hat she wears constantly, perched at a rakish angle dipped slightly over one eye, her hair caught into some kind of simple style—tucked up beneath the crown—her ears partially covered—the tops—and the lower section uncovered. Her presence startled me. She looked up at me, smiled, and quickly glanced downward again.

I spoke to her—quickly—telling her we would leave immediately. I finished speaking on the telephone with Roger—the Foreman—who suggested I spend the weekend as I pleased and report back for work on Monday.

I was sure Janine was holding a solution of amphetamine and was anxious to turn on. She had some vague idea about cashing checks. The plan was completely obscure and we ended walking—14th Street – 7th Avenue – Sheridan Square. We stopped in a diner for coffee, ice cream and a piece of pastry. I went into the men's room first and then she went into the ladies' room. We both turned on shots of amphetamine – leaving – strolling – talking – finally taking a cab to 34th Street – continuing to walk and talk over toward the east side – across Park Avenue – over to Third Avenue – down 3rd – eventually deciding to ride back downtown – to see Freude and John Wieners. It was a truly great evening and Janine had been open, talking, explaining much of what previously only confused me. The running around from spot to spot – observing the night – speaking of each

130

other – of people – love – Bill Heinie – Victor – Peter – Fernando. At last reaching the loft where Fernando began making decided announcements about the immediate future. Telling Janine it had become necessary to vacate the loft and that he was turning over a new leaf. No more drugs. He was leaving the scene until he felt he had regained strength to resume painting. The atmosphere was tense and I began feeling my fatigue intensely. Speaking briefly with Janine — suggesting she consider returning home to Jersey for a short while — feeling it better I depart I bid goodnight and began walking over toward the east side, intending to return to John Weiners' and sleep.

My eyes felt heavy and my skin had become a shroud of exposed nerve ends — quivering and undulating waves of sensitivity. My mouth was extremely dry and I felt it was oozing musk. My walk took me through a short span of Washington Square, up toward University Place then over to 8th Street until it becomes St. Mark's at 3rd Avenue — where I encountered a young man named Joe who had been introduced to me as a connection for practically anything – pot, goofballs, amphetamine pills of various kinds and heroin. He was sitting at the foot of some steps leading up into a house partly given over to a small theater group, a huge sign in shades of lavender with white lettering partially covering one side of the front. We greeted each other and he asked me if I was interested in copping. I said I was providing there wouldn't be a big hassle. He said there wouldn't be — that as a matter of fact he was waiting to get in touch with his men or one of his boys at the very moment, that he was going into the house, where a party was underway, in order to pick up a couple of his friends, maybe stay a few minutes, and then cut to where his man would undoubtedly be on the scene. He suggested I join him in visiting the party, arguing against my immediate rejection of the idea. I explained I dislike parties, particularly if I am unacquainted with the people. Also I was much too tired — in fact exhausted — to even think about it, but I didn't mind waiting on the steps while he went in – took care of whatever business he had in mind. We argued for several minutes and finally he decided to go in without me. He pushed the doorbell and was admitted, while I settled down comfortably 131 on the steps to wait.

It was a warm, almost sultry, night – and people were stirring about the streets listlessly. A couple of spade cats cut by – a woman, rather strangely dressed – wearing several strands of beads around her neck, and several bracelets on her arm she seemed annoyed with as she passed. She shook her arm rather violently and then began adjusting the bracelets with her hand—first taking a huge handbag she was carrying and placing it firmly up under her armpit, pressing it against her body. As occupied as she was with her jewelry, handbag and putting herself aright, she did look at me—sharply—quickly glancing away as our eyes met. Several times taxis passed. I was just beginning to feel relaxed and enjoying my freshly-lit cigarette when my name was called out and, looking upward, there was my acquaintance leaning out one of the upper windows. He called down for me to come on in and join the scene. Several of the cats he wanted to see were milling around, and it was pointless for me to sit outside. "Come on man, don't be a drag—fall in. We won't stay long. I want to make a couple of phone calls. Then straight away to the man." Suddenly it did seem pointless my sitting outside and I agreed to join him.

I climbed the steps and as I reached the top the door buzzer began sounding and I opened the door and stepped in.

A lovely teardrop-shaped crystal chandelier hung in the center of the entrance hall. The floor was painted a bright venetian red. One wall consisted nearly completely of an inset mirror. A great wide gracious-appearing staircase led upward into the upper regions of the house. I began mounting the stairs and my friend began calling down to me, telling me to come up, man – keep climbing – it is up here at the top. Finally reaching him, he began telling me we wouldn't stay long, there wasn't any pot, three girls who rented the house were giving the party, some of his best friends were there but there were innumerable people he didn't know – we could have a can of beer – not to worry – we would cut out soon.

I had little opportunity to observe the general plan of the house—getting a quick impression of many rooms and doors, little side staircases leading even further upward, and in one instance the impression of a split-level room.

There were people everywhere—in groups, standing alone, sitting on floors – chairs – chests; in couples, some making love, some laying back in each other's arms. Several girls were clustered around a phonograph, listening in rapt attention to a Lena Horne rendition of some torch song. Beer cans were scattered in every direction. Upon first encountering the full blast of this gathering of people I was immediately conscious of the youth of everyone. I didn't at any time before departing see the entire crowd at once, but I am sure there was no one over twenty-five years of age.

As people became aware of my presence I became exceedingly uncomfortable. There were no friendly faces, no smiles of welcome, no pleasant greetings, and—worse —an increasing wariness of me, so that at one point I am quite sure I was being stared at by thirty of forty pairs of eyes, all registering open curiosity, hostility and rejection. All this before anyone had spoken to me, heard my name, knew for sure I was alive and not an animated dummy somehowbeingdraggedintotheirmidstfortheiramusement.

The scene was kaleidoscopic and I was surprised when suddenly one of the girls took form, looking at me with great paranoia-filled eyes, then calling sharply to my friend "Please Joe, let me speak to you"—pulling him after her into a small side room.

My whole feeling was of being trapped and of some-how escaping as soon as possible. I had turned toward the door through which we had entered to discover several young guys standing in a group—obviously discussing me— almost in front of the door. My mind was beginning to whirl, sending out thoughts—reactions, impressions, feelings of fear, confusion—like the sputtering sparks of a pinwheel.

I was standing in a reception hall with rooms opening off in three directions. Several people had gathered in the room—two half-reclining against a large chest of drawers occupying the largest wall. Two young men were standing in between two of the doorways. I had crossed the room around these people and was just about to follow the young woman and Joe. They had gone just beyond the third doorway, and I could hear the girl whispering in excited rushes of heavy breath to Joe, who would make some mumbled reply. Somehow feelings of guilt swept over me, 133 and for the moment I believed it necessary to speak to the girl—explaining my desire to leave, my not having wanted to invade the party in the first place. Just as I was about to follow into the room after them they reappeared, and I immediately began talking to the girl, telling her I wanted to leave and would do so at once. She became intensely embarrassed—blurting out some statement about my being alright, I should stay, I wasn't to feel uncomfortable, etc. Joe kept interrupting her to assure me everything was great—stay a little while, he was going to speak with his buddies, it would only take a few minutes, then we would go. Meanwhile the girl slipped past me, disappearing into the group in the main room.

Suddenly one of the cats near the door we had entered through spoke up, looking contemptuously at me, saying "you are fucked up man." At first I was surprised at his rudeness and his language and then I was annoyed—annoyed with the whole stinking mess, plus the utter stupidity of this opinionated ape who stood looking so righteous, mouthing words he didn't even understand at me—someone he had never set eyes on before. "What exactly do you mean by fucked up?" I asked him. "Perhaps you will explain." "Oh you know, man, fucked up." Just then one of the other fellows standing near moved over toward me, saying "What's your name?" I told him my name and he repeated it after me, saying "Huncke—what kind of a name is that?" I spelled it for him, explaining it is German. "German!" he almost screeched at me, "German, a lousy Nazi. Well man, I'm a Jew. It was you bastard Germans sent my grandmother, grandfather, relatives of my friends to the gas chambers. I hate Germans."

My whole being filled with sadness and the only thought I could formulate in my conscious mind was that it was tragic he would use anything as crude as racial hatred as a means of inflating his ego in the presence of his friends and as a means of attempting to humiliate me. I was so completely stymied, all I could think to say was, "Wow man—how old are you?"

Gradually during this exchange several more people were crowding the doorways. Everyone was talking at once 134 and I was really frightened that I was to be—at the very least—severely beaten.

Yet I wasn't entirely alone. Looking around me, I became aware of four or five young cats gathering around Joe, who looked at me with warmth and understanding. Obviously the friends Joe had come to see. Beautiful young men, who quickly began introducing themselves—Richie – Don – John – Bert—telling me not to pay any attention to these other people. Calling for beer—trying to ease the tension a little.

Still—my beligerent acquaintance was not to be stopped. Raising his voice, he began saying, "This party needs more girls. I want more girls." Looking at me, he said, "What do you want more of?"

My response was immediate. "Peace," I said. "Peace."

"Peace?" he replied, "peace shit. What you want more of is boys with nice long joints. I know what you are—you're a fag. That's what you are—a goddamned fag."

Joe and Richie both spoke up, saying "Man, you're crazy. Huncke's no fag. Wow—how wrong can you get." I was utterly speechless—unable to say anything—seething with self-loathing because I didn't raise my hands to this man who dared try and belittle and degrade me. Yet also aware of pity for this sick, insecure—in all probability— frustrated homosexual.

Meanwhile positions had been shifted and Joe was now at the door holding it open calling his friends, saying "Come on, Huncke, let's split."

Perhaps the very act of our making an exit at that particular moment helped avert what might very easily have been a slam-bang free-for-all. I was glad to leave. Glad to be free from what had threatened to be a violent display. I was rather shocked to think my appearance alone could be the cause of so devastating a situation—one filled with hate and paranoia.

On the street with Joe and his friends, listening to their discussion of what had happened and why, I regained my composure.

Joe was full of explanations about how square they all were—just schoolkids trying to come on like men of the world, showing off in front of their girls. Richie was a bit more perceptive in my opinion, saying that obviously it wasn't all me—part of it being Joe and some of his unpre- 135 dictable escapades of the past the girls knew of, and some of the fellows—and the fear he had planned to louse up their evening some way by bringing in a complete outsider.

We all went back to the Village to Macdougal Street near the Fat Black Pussy Cat where we hung around until Joe made my connect for me. I left him and his friends still talking about ways and means of evening up the score at the party.

Walking along alone, thinking about all that had happened, I realized I should have been capable in some manner of having spread understanding and trust—a sense of peace. I was filled with shame because it had not been in my power—or, if it had been, I had not recognized the way to use the ability to open their eyes to beauty.

THE LAW OF RETRIBUTION

Some people hold grudges for a long time—perhaps until they die—and there is never a rest from the moment the grudge takes shape in their mind until they have retaliated in a similar manner to the one who they believe is responsible, or have evened up the score as one might say. They are on the alert to gain revenge—quite frequently working out elaborate plans and schemes to serve their purpose—and more often than not it doesn't matter to what extent the other person is guilty. The whole idea of retribution, or of gaining revenge, applies not only to a grudge but to any situation wherein one of two people, or groups of people, has gained or—supposedly unfairly—taken advantage of the other.

It is all stupid and a decided waste of energy, and is one of the worst aspects of human relationships. But, regardless, it does occur, and like all ideas resulting from the idea of competition there are certain rules of rather rigid nature which affect the entire concept so that, as an example, if one partner steals from the other—or in some way deserts the other, or lies, or cheats—in the world of hustlers, and particularly among those of Latin extraction and background, a knife is often used – frequently a gun. And if the two people involved are male, a so-called man usually—at the very least—promises himself he'll knock the shit out of the bastard the next time there is an opportunity.

When I first began hanging around the underworld I was cautious and careful of fulfilling—or attempting to fulfill—my obligations in any of my dealings where I had a partner. And the first time I held out—the result of an error of calculation on my part and an honest mistake—I was ashamed and extremely worried that perhaps the discrepancy would be discovered and, in the vernacular, I'd get my head handed to me. Nothing ever came of it, and when finally I was confronted with a situation—this time with a new partner—where I could gain at the other's expense, it 137 took little argument with my conscience to decide to go ahead, and again I had no trouble. Then came the time where I knew beforehand there would be no way of covering up and my act would be considered an out-and-out burn, and in my heart I knew the only way of evening up—eventually —would be through an act of violence on the part of my partner. I took the gamble of our never meeting again—or of meeting so much later the sting of the injury would be dissipated, and I could perhaps talk my way out of the worst of the consequences—and I went ahead and in a sense got away with it. Although we did meet again much later, all that happened was a verbal tongue-lashing. It is alright to burn one's victims as long as they can be referred to as marks, but never—**never**—burn the guy you work with and who is your partner. Where the line of justification for an act of treachery in one instance—which ceases to be justifiable in another instance—exists is a moot question and one, honestly speaking, I've never understood.

Be that as it may, there is a law of retribution—and recently it caught up with me.

At the time I made the choice—or acted according to the dictates of my desire—I had been the partner of a Spanish-American cat for a period of several months, and had known him about three years. When we became partners we began dealing junk together, and although he was experienced in the business I was quite green and unaware of much of what might be required of me—as to conduct when unexpectedly I discovered I was working someone else's territory, or when I was held up at knife point and told to give up my junk or get cut, or the various hypes I'd be subjected to. I soon discovered my co-worker was very unscrupulous as to his manner of dealing with me, and although there was never anything I could use to explain— without having to qualify in some involved way why I felt cheated—I did in a sense come out on the short end of the deal. Still—in a sense—I was treated, all the same, fairly, and perhaps could have behaved differently in the final analysis and avoided a very unpleasant experience.

We had been together several months. It was winter and through some thoroughly high-handed manipulation 138 on the part of my partner I was suddenly without a place of my own to live, and was living with him and his girl and feeling disgusted and completely trapped. I became somewhat desperate about what the future might hold in store were I to continue as I had been. One cold, cold morning I got up, and when I went to cook up my usual fix my partner began complaining about the amount of stuff being used, and ordered me to cut down. I felt that since I was running the risk of being arrested at any time, the least I could have out of the deal was as much stuff as I liked, and I was annoyed with his complaint. Therefore it took very little debating the issue when, later that morning, I had eighteen bags of stuff in my possession—all the merchandise we had between us—and I stopped to visit a young woman I knew and she suggested I kick my habit—she would help me with the money to get to Lexington, Kentucky where I could enter the hospital—to decide in favor of taking her up on the plan. I simply remained with her all day until it was time to catch the bus—frequently shooting up and taking the rest with me, shooting the last of it upon my arrival in Lexington. I had shot up the eighteen bags in less than 24 hours.

I remained out of the city several months, and by the time I returned I learned he had been arrested and was serving time. He was gone two years.

He was released not long ago.

I have always known there would be a day of reckoning and have mentioned it to several of our mutual associates. He had told everyone and—although several people thought he'd forget—I was sure he wouldn't. I was convinced he would have to prove to his friends, if nothing else, no one gets away with crossing him.

We met walking along the street. I had paused a moment to speak with an acquaintance, and as I turned around—there he was. He walked up to me, grabbed me by my arm pulling me up close to him, and sort of forced me to accompany him down the street, meanwhile daring me to make an explanation. Suddenly, after walking a short distance, he swung his fist up into my face, cracking me on the lip – continuing to walk, again hitting me – finally hitting me again, threatening to cut me. There was nothing I could say. From his point of view he was perfectly justified and certainly wouldn't have understood any of my abstract reasoning were I to have attempted explaining. In his eyes he had been lenient. I understood and was grateful he hadn't cut me with a knife.

We parted on somewhat agreeable terms, and at the time I thought it wiser of me to continue avoiding him as much as possible.

I was ashamed of my behavior and promised myself to act always in the future in a manner where I would never again knowingly cause someone to feel the need to retaliate or to put in effect the so-called law of retribution.

THE SAVIOUR

I have always thought of myself as a good talker and once I talked a man out of shooting another man, although I didn't succeed in talking him out of his violence. He was a man filled with frustration and constant anxiety which would erupt into great outbursts of denunciation toward anyone he felt at the particular time had treated him—as he understood it—unjustly, and was apt at such times to resort to physical assault. He wasn't of large stature but possessed an abundance of energy and could, if not checked immediately, inflict much pain. Fortunately these outbursts occurred seldom, and although verbally he was constantly attacking his supposed enemies it was only on rare occasions he gave vent to his more violent impulses.

At the time I am speaking of he was in between steady women and had been shacking up with a girl who was attracted by young boys. She was something of a whore, though she would go to great ends to deny it and preferred having people think she was being kept by some old man that went to sea who sent her an allotment. She had been making the 42nd Street scene for quite some time, and I had gotten to know her thru one of the boys she had picked up.

Just how they met is rather vague, but it seems the main attraction was a certain satisfaction each derived comparing notes concerning their prior loves. He was just getting over being jilted and she had just gotten rid of her most recent boy because she had decided he was queer—since he didn't wish to go down on her, which was what she liked best.

They were living in a small pad on West 15th Street and we all three would sit around smoking pot while they did most of the talking. Both sort of considered me a harmless friend each could confide in, and frequently called upon me to settle disputes.

He was very possessive and had threatened to beat her if he caught her making it with anyone else. She was always reassuring and called him her man.

One evening he came in unexpectedly and caught her balling a young kid. I was with him and knew the kid from the Square and managed to get the kid out of the pad before too much trouble developed.

She was contrite and begged forgiveness, explaining that he hadn't laid her the previous night or given her head, and of course he knew how hot-natured she was, and besides, the kid had practically forced her. He admitted to being indirectly responsible—yet no goddamned punk was going to lay his old lady and get away with it. He rushed over and grabbed his gun which was a gift from his brother who had brought it back from overseas, and with me in pursuit rushed out into the night to find the no-good son-of-a-bitch and blow his brains out.

We headed more or less toward 42nd Street—stopping at various bars en route. He kept up a steady tirade against the poor kid until I could only hope that by this time the kid was somewhere at the other end of Brooklyn.

At three in the morning at the corner of 43rd Street and 8th Avenue just off the corner heading toward 9th Avenue we ran into him.

It was a slightly cool morning and the few people on the streets were rushing along either toward the subway or bars or just to keep warm. The three of us standing in the reflection of the streetlamp must have made a strange and frightening picture. The one pale and shaking—pleading not to be hurt. Another livid with rage—filled with confusion—tense and ready to kill. And the other keenly aware of the drama and horrified—talking, talking, talking against events over which there seemed to be no control, and telling first one and then the other to keep cool. Beseeching the very atmosphere to help prevent the pulling of the trigger. It was a very tense and explosive moment and all I could do was talk. Asking, explaining, reasoning, constantly pointing out the stupidity of the situation and the sheer horror of the whole scene. It seemed that gradually things began to relax and that suddenly it was over.

We spoke of the incident many times and later he was glad—sincerely glad—he had calmed down, and has frequently thanked me for my talking.

I no longer know where he is for sure though via the so-called grapevine he is now in Cleveland, still angry and lonely.

FRISKY

The last few weeks, on occasion I've had reason to visit Don Neald's and Jimmy's pad on Bleecker Street. Tom Sato—an oriental cat about forty or forty-five years of age—actually set the place up originally and still lives there with Don and Jimmy. It is a strange place, consisting of three rooms opening up from the front—intended as a store—above street level one flight up and running to the back room, where at some point someone decided to make a sort of built-in wall seat to run the full width of the back wall, setting it back under a pair of arches that extended in front of it about three feet. To one side is a plain brick wall with a huge iron pikestaff caught on it at an angle. Opposite is a window looking out to the courtyard, with heavy red plush drapes. Between these and the next window is a table, a mirror hanging above it and a lamp with a Japanese shade. Along the wall next to the bare brick area is a large double studio couch with end tables; next a chest of drawers and a closet. The colors in the room are somber browns and dark greens and reds. There is an air of the old and decayed in the atmosphere, and one would hardly be surprised to discover at least one haunted sister—pale faced—communing with the dead, or perchance a stuffed owl—burning—and a coffin.

At the time I am speaking of, several unusually beautiful young girls were staying there along with Don, Jim and Tom Sato. From what little I was able to learn of their background they grew up together—all about the same age: the oldest 21 or 22 and the youngest 18. Terry, Penny, Barbara, Dexie and Frisky. There is one other beautiful child, fourteen, who occasionally fell in, stayed a while, maybe turned on a shot of amphets, and then disappeared into the city outside.

The night El Flower and I put Deborah on the bus to California we returned downtown to the location of the Catholic Worker's headquarters, where we spent a short 143 time speaking with a friend of El's. As we left, El suggested we try and cop a bag of horse—asking me if I knew where we might accomplish same. I immediately thought of Sato's. We walked over to the Bowery at Delancey and headed up toward Bleecker. En route we ran into Nick and a friend of his. I spoke briefly with Nick, who said he was headed to Sato's and to pick him up there. But we followed closely behind and entered almost at the same time. I said hello to everyone and El acknowledged introductions, his eyes lighting up at the scene, darting around the rooms observing the girls. Frisky was half reclining on the divan talking to a young cat—Jerry—I had only seen once before. Everyone else was located in the back room. As we entered, Don raised up and asked if either of us had any amphets. When we said no he sighed and fell back down, grumbling about not having turned on all day. He said, "Wow—all these people cutting in and out—this ain't no shooting gallery." Nickie and his friend proceeded to get straight, cooking up their shit. Barbara was in the process of getting dressed, and at the moment was applying some kind of eye makeup. Penny had moved over to watch Nickie. I sat down in a chair facing the couch. Terry was curled up alongside Don. Looking toward the back, I saw Tom Sato apparently sleeping on the wall seat. A spread of some kind, partially obscuring him from view, hung in one of the arches. Don was still muttering unintelligible sounds, every other one a grunt or snort, taking on form such as amphets – tired – chaos – confusion – too many people.

Suddenly, looking directly at him, I said, "Hey man, are you complaining because I fell in? If you don't want me cutting in, all that is necessary is you say so." He answered by saying, "Well you know, Huncke, it isn't you exactly, but strangers." I answered immediately, saying "Are you referring to Flower? Wow – he's good people. Not only that – I am usually careful who I introduce, and to whom I introduce. Also there are few people at this point any cooler than me." Don said, "I know, man." Just then Penny spoke up, saying "It's just – Don doesn't want so many people falling in at once." I didn't say anything – looking the scene over – thinking fuck these people – or how hung up can they get. If I'd had amphets nothing at all would have been mentioned other than "Great – can we turn on? Have you enough so we can all get a shot?"

Meanwhile El spoke to Nickie asking him if as soon as he had finished he would cop a bag of schmeck for us. Nickie said yes. Just then Jimmy walked by and, looking at me, said, "You look annoyed Huncke." I didn't answer. El turned to me and began questioning me about whether or not I trusted Nickie. I started to say "Yes, of course" and then it occurred to me the whole routine was pretty fucking stupid. "Shit no – I don't trust anybody. There ain't no mother-fucker alive I believe in. Everybody stinks." Jimmy interrupted to say "What's the matter man?" I replied, "Nothing, except people. Fuck people. The more I know of them the less I want to be around them." At the moment I was irritated with Don and his whole stupid attitude. It annoyed me he should dare have opinions of me, especially since he knew me not at all personally and was only mouthing things he had heard said.

Nickie finished shooting up, picked up the money from El and cut out, saying he'd be back as soon as possible. After he left his friend came over and joined us, saying "My name is Johnny Walsh." He began telling us of himself and of how he had just beaten a federal rap. It had taken two years and a lot of money. The talk became general, every-one speaking of one thing or another—mostly of drugs. Someone mentioned having turned on synthetic cocaine the night before, also making a comment about wishing some were available at the moment. A couple of hours before El had given me a large bag containing just what they were talking about. El looked at me and said, "You got it with you, man?" I nodded yes and he spoke aloud, saying "Look, I don't know what the stuff is, but Huncke and I have something that is supposed to be artificial or synthetic coke. If you want to use some, you're welcome." Don jumped up and said, "Yes man, I would sure appreciate shooting some up." Johnny Walsh asked to see the stuff, saying he'd like to try a little, asking me if I was going to shoot some also. I really don't like the idea of synthetic anything—much less cocaine—but I was feeling nervous and it occurred to me possibly I'd get a lift. I said "Yes. In fact, let me go first. I've had some experience with it once 145 or twice before and know just about what to put in the spoon." I cooked up, drew the stuff into the dropper and shot up. For a moment nothing, and then the strange freezing sensation in my mouth – and on the tip of my tongue and around the gums – and a momentary rush to the pit of my stomach. I felt a bit ill for a moment and then all was well. Everyone was watching me. They began asking questions about whether or not I felt it – if I liked it – if it was good. I shrugged my shoulders, saying "Yes – no – it's OK – not really great – just a slight rush – over with now – nothing is happening." Barbara said, "You look happy. I'm going to try some." Meanwhile Johnny Walsh had taken over and was in the process of preparing himself a fix. He proceeded to take off, saying—after he had removed the needle—"Man, I don't feel anything." Don was next, then Barbara. Penny and Jimmy went out for soda and cigarettes. El was getting restless. He had an appointment at the Metro coffee house he didn't want to miss. He said for me to wait for Nickie and we would meet later at Noah and Paul's. As he was walking toward the front, Frisky passed him, asking if it would be alright for her to take a little shot too. El answered "of course" and she came on through into the back room. As she passed me she smiled, then stopped a moment, extending her hands to me. She said, "Let's see how strong you are. Here, put up your hand." I took both her hands in mine and we exerted strength and pressure to see which could force the other to bend their arms. She was quite strong. We both began laughing. "You're stronger than I thought," I said. She looked pleased. Suddenly she withdrew her hands and moved over to the table with the works and the stuff. She paused a moment before the mirror, pulling her dress into position, fluffing her long black hair a little around her ears, twisting one way and another in order to see herself at different angles. She was half smiling, looking pleased. Johnny Walsh was sitting at the table and she asked him to please fix her a shot. She continued standing fussing with her appearance—putting lipstick on, smoothing it down on her mouth with her little finger, brushing a bright turquoise-blue dress trimmed with orange-and-black bands around the neck and the bottom of the skirt. 146 She had low-cut dark blue sneakers on her feet and bent down to loosen the laces of one which she kicked off, grimacing and remarking about a blister on the back of her heel. Johnny had prepared her shot and she sat down to tie up. Seeing her, for the moment the thought flashed through my mind—perhaps she shouldn't take very much, if any—and then it was gone. I was still very annoyed with Don, and besides, apparently they all had been shooting together for quite some time and she probably knew what she was doing. Also Nickie was overdue and I was becoming bugged waiting. Barbara was sitting opposite me and Penny and Jimmy had just returned with bottles of Coca-Cola and packages of cigarettes.

I saw Barbara, who was looking in the direction of Frisky and John, suddenly stiffen—a look of fright on her face. As I turned to look I heard her gasp and let out a little scream. I saw Frisky raise up halfway out of the chair she had been sitting in, fling her arms out stiffly, throw her head back, spin to one side and fall to the floor in a state of convulsive spasms—her whole body rigid and quivering. Johnny leaped from his seat and Jimmy rushed across to her side, calling her name. Bending down they began trying to life her, turning her first to one side then the other. The girls all began talking at once, making suggestions. Everyone started moving around. The two fellows succeeded in lifting her off the floor and moving her into a half-reclining position on the couch or the bed where, one on either side, they tried holding her down. She was breathing in gasps from deep in her throat through gurgling saliva. She was choking on the bile accumulated in her throat. Every now and then she would partially come to and strain to raise up, her eyes wide open staring straight ahead. They continued to hold her in position until she would pass out again.

Meanwhile Tom Sato had leaped from his bed, thrown on his hat and coat and rushed out, presumably to try and find out what the antidote for the stuff might be. Barbara and I had collected the works together. I arranged mine and placed them in my pocket. I had tried to make several suggestions about how to handle the girl and was either not heard or simply ignored, and besides—I was not at all sure about what should be done. Jimmy had called me a couple of times asking me if I knew exactly how to handle 147 the situation and all I could reply was—no.

I decided to leave. I spoke quietly to Barbara, asking her to please let me out and to close and lock the door after I left. Barbara was shaken and her eyes were filled with tears. "They should try and let her cough up the bile and saliva," she said. "She is choking this way and no one will listen to me." There was nothing I could say except, "Don't worry baby, she'll be alright." As Barbara let me out she repeated her statement and said "I know I'm right." I told her to take care and stepped out onto the street. I walked straight home to the apartment to find El already there and waiting. I explained what had happened and he became upset, exclaiming—"Oh man, what a drag – wow – that poor chick."

In a short time the three girls—Terry, Penny and Barbara—arrived across the hall at Margot and Nickie's, saying as they came in "She is dead." I was shocked and asked them to explain about what had happened after I left. They told me finally Tom Sato and Nickie, who had returned, helped get her into a taxi. Her pulse had stopped beating and she had turned blue. Someone had called a policeman explaining that she had committed suicide. I don't know any further details except she was reported a suicide and dead on arrival.

CRUISER ON AVENUE B

Another new notebook, and at the moment not at all sure of exactly what I want to write about and suppose probably the best thing I could start with is an experience that oc-curred about an hour ago—a brief encounter with two police officers in a police-car or cruiser who called me over to ask me questions. I had known almost positively they were interested in me upon my first becoming aware of their presence. Suddenly glancing to the side while walking slowly along Avenue B at the time my attention somewhat abstractedly drew toward the entrance way of the Charles Theatre or movie house, just beneath the marquee so that also there was an element of surprise. As I watched, still strolling, their obvious interest in me — and there could be no doubt — the officer behind the wheel, the driver, was speaking of me. As he half turned his head toward his companion and continued slowly moving alongside of me, while by then, disconcerted by their intrusion I was inwardly attempting to appear nonchalant and not in the least troubled by any interest the police could have in my most ordinary life and the dull and spotless course of my daily existence. And on another level, swept through with thoughts of my appearance in the pale light of the slightly misty grey early morning, the strange, rather drained color of my skin and the several red colored sores on my face (one on the tip of my nose, another over one cheek bone, both almost like rouge spots), my hair combed and windblown and my eyes large, brown, near-sighted pools of dilation. All of this was accompanied with momentary flashes of doubt, very likely the possibility of having something of an illegal nature on my person, suddenly and momentarily frightened me. Then, thinking about my pockets – from my wallet and moving rapidly from pocket to pocket and finally, as I relaxed, sure there was nothing – and at the instant they motioned for me to approach, I had ventured another glance in their direction. After all, I've almost as much right to look at 149 them as they have to observe me. They called "Hey — come over here a moment." I remember a half stick of pot in one of my jacket pockets. For a moment, fear filled me to capacity. I immediately began to walk toward them, reaching for my back pocket and my wallet which contained my identification. (I use my passport as a rule even though it expired last October and isn't the best I.D. to have as a result.)

When I reached their side of the street and when I could speak to them so they could hear me without my having to raise my voice, I spoke, saying "Is there something wrong? Would you like to see my identification?" and handed same to them. I was on the side next to the driver. I looked straight at him, taking in his insignia, which I am never really sure about, never having forced myself to recognize their symbols of rank, thusly never knowing if I'm speaking with a captain, a lieutenent or a sergeant or man of simple rank. He was a young man in his late twenties or early thirties; I'd guess about 32 years of age. His facial features were inoffensive although he bore stern and mean demeanor. His expression was full of surprise and hostility. He looked me up and down, his eyes stopping as they reached mine, and I could feel his search for an indication of my being a drug user. He asked me if I hadn't just handed something over to a man I had spoken with back up the street. At first, I immediately denied any knowledge of what he was talking about, and then I did recall stopping to speak with Victor, to whom I had handed a slip of paper with an address and telephone number written on it.

ARRESTED

The sun blazed down on the ice-wrapped city. People pushed thru the wind-swept streets, rapidly seeking the warmth of entranceways, subways, restaurants, buildings and, anywhere out of the wind, huddled in coats, jackets, sweaters, mittens and gloves. The sputtering of the radiator finally penetrated my sleep and after getting out of bed and looking out the window, I dreaded the thought of having to go out into the day. It was late in the morning, but somewhat early in the day for me to be awake. I had taken a fix just before going to sleep, saving part of what I had in my possession awakening. I was broke and had to take a suit, part of some loot taken from a car the previous week and saved for just an emergency as I now faced: broke and the cold too severe to get out and hustle (and my junk almost gone) to the pawnshop. I fixed, dressed, and, taking the suit from the closet, rushed down the stairs and across the street to the nearest pawnshop, which was where I had pawned several items from the same loot of which the suit belonged. I threw the suit up on the counter and asked for ten dollars. After examing the suit, the man behind the counter told me to wait a minute: he turned and walked toward the back of the shop. This wasn't exactly an unusual procedure and it was with surprise and a sinking of the heart that I suddenly became aware of three men standing behind me. The man behind the counter had returned and was pointing a finger at me, saying "this is the one." Two of the men stepped forward on either side of me and quickly began frisking me and asking me questions about where I had gotten the suit, where I lived and if I thought I was a wise-guy and telling me this was a pinch and I was sure unlucky since they just happened to be there checking on the stuff that I had hocked before.

"This man is the owner" they said, pointing to the third man, "and we're going to see to it that he presses charges. You'll probably go away for a long time. Are you a junky? You look like one."

ALVAREZ

I first saw him when I climbed into the patrol-wagon. He was sitting well toward the back, all drawn up into a tight knot, his head sunk between his shoulders, arms wrapped around his body, knees pressed together and pulled up toward his chin so that only the tips of his toes supported his weight. He was wearing a trench coat several sizes too large, which hung in loose folds around him, the bottom dragging on the floor, and a misshapen black felt hat with a wide brim, pulled down over his forehead. He was thin; almost skeletal and skin of a pale jaundice yellow color. His face was skull-like with enormous eye sockets. The eyes were large and black-brown, glazed and staring straight ahead. He was shivering, and as I settled into my seat, he began shaking and shuddering; his whole body jerked convulsively. Tears glistened at the corners of his eyes. His nose was running; a thin drop of mucus hung from the tip. He was emitting a strange, almost wail-like sound and occasionally groaning, babbling to himself in Spanish interspersed with broken English of which the words "I'm sick...I'm sick...I'm sick" was all I could understand. Suddenly he vomited, regurgitating globs of green bile, and fell back afterward on the seat, moaning.

We were going down to police headquarters to be finger printed, photographed, put thru the show-up, and formally booked and charged with our respective crimes, examined and thoroughly frisked, interviewed, then sent thru a cold shower and finally assigned to a floor and a cell in the City Prison to wait trial. I couldn't help but speculate about how they expected to get the man thru the entire procedure (which is an ordeal even when one is in good health) without his collapsing completely.

We were the only two prisoners in the wagon. The cop who was sitting guard over us kept making remarks to me about how disgusting it was to see anyone in such a condition. "The poor sonofabitch would be better off dead. I ain't got no sympathy for you guys. Why do you do it? There ain't nothing worse than junk. How come you ain't like him — you're a junkie too ain't you? Oh well, you'll probably get like that later."

The ride downtown seemed interminable and I was glad when we stopped and the cop said "End of the line. Let's go. Come on — no stalling." I was still feeling fairly good, but he had to be dragged and cuffed alongside the head before he could manage to stagger and half fall out of the wagon and down the stairs past the newspaper reporters and photographers into headquarters, where we were separated. At headquarters things move slowly and it wasn't until much later in the day that I saw him again.

At headquarters, I was assigned to a cell where I waited until they called me out to be printed and photographed, after which I was taken upstairs to the show-up and then down to the courtroom where I appeared before a judge who decided what bail was to be set — then over to the city prison.

Sometimes, if a junky is very sick or if the detective handling the case is afraid the junky is apt to get sick in the courtroom (something the judges frown upon), arrangements are made for the junky to have a shot. Such must have happened with the fellow who had ridden down with me, because he was certainly in much better shape when they led him into the bullpen, where we were to wait until assignment to our regular cells. Finally our names were called and we were led over to the shower room where we stripped our clothes and left them in a pile. Each piece was closely examined, seams were carefully felt for concealed needles or stashes of junk. The shoes were banged on the floor and inspected for false heels or soles, while we stood in a shower of cold water or waited shivering until the frisk was over. After dressing we were led before a doctor and given a cursory examination. We were asked how long we had used junk and what kind. The sick man was behind me in line, and while talking to the doctor, asked for a fix. He was told, "There will be no fix for you. This is jail, not a sanitarium. You kick — cold turkey."

We were both sent to the eighth floor. They try and keep the junkies all together and his cell was two down 153 from mine.

The cells in the city prison were originally designed to accomodate one, but in the last few years have been used to hold two. Each cell now contains an upper and lower bunk, a toilet, a small washbasin, a stool or seat which lets down from the wall, and a small square metal shelf or ledge which serves as a table. Each prisoner is issued three blankets (not always clean), a sheet, a pillow case and a towel. The bunks consist of a set of springs. There are no mattresses or pallets and sometimes no pillows. Therefore it is necessary to use at least one of the blankets as a sort of pad over the springs. Before there were two springs in each cell, and when it became necessary to put two men in a cell, one or the other was forced to sleep on the floor.

Each floor is broken up into four sections and alphabetically designated A section, B section, C section, D section. In each section there is a flats, the main floor row of cells and a tier, or the row of cells immediately above those on the flats. There are approximately 48 to 50 cells in each section. The cells face a sort of well which runs the full length of each row, extending as far over as a catwalk and surrounding the entire floor. Large full length panels of small frosted glass windows extend around each floor. Once one is on the inside, one sees daylight but never a glimpse of the outside.

The cells are opened early in the morning, usually shortly after breakfast, which is served on trays and brought to the cell by trustees. And regardless of how one feels, it is required the prisoners gather out on the flats and remain there until it is time for the midday meal when they return to their cells for an hour and come out again for what is termed afternoon recreation. This routine never varies and is only an additional discomfort for addicts who are sick and weak, and in most instances unable to stand for long and who must sit with head bowed over a long table flanking the side of the catwalk (if lucky) or end up sitting on the floor. The cells are closed and one can't get back in to lie down until the next lockup.

I had managed to get through my first day without getting sick. I had fixed only a short time before being
154 arrested so that it wasn't until the following day that the

real misery began. I had been put into a cell with a fellow who had been there almost two weeks and who was over the worst of his kicking. Probably the worst thing about kicking a habit cold turkey is being unable to sleep. I have talked to men who have gone three or four weeks without sleep. Nothing is quite so agonizing as lying on a set of springs which cut into you no matter how you try and pad them from squeaking with each breath you take and are lopsided and frequently broken.

The first night I slept fitfully, becoming familiar with the night sounds of a prison — the guard passing with flashlight and jingling keys, farts, snoring, groaning, sleep talk, flushing toilets, phone ringings, muffled conversations, closing doors, church chimes, traffic, shouts on the streets below and the constant noise of people sick and unable to sleep, moving and adjusting, seeking the more comfortable position.

My companion of the morning (whose name I had learned was Alvarez) cried, groaned, stopped the guard, begging to see a doctor and asking for something to ease his pain. He called for Maria, Rita, Lola, banged against the bars and was told to "Shut up, for Christ's sake. Lay down you bastard — there are others trying to sleep. Come out swinging in the morning you punk bastard. You ain't any sicker than I am" by other prisoners. When I saw him the following morning, he looked like a Zombie. He staggered out of the cell with a blanket wrapped shawl fashion around his shoulders, his hair hanging down over his forehead and eyes, shivering and shaking and wracked with dry heaving, unable to vomit anymore because there was no longer even green bile in his stomach. He kind of collapsed into a heap on the floor and remained there the entire morning while prisoners wanting to pass him simply stepped over him. Once, he managed to get up long enough to wander down toward the end of the flats and call to the guard on duty, asking to see a doctor. The guard told him to "get the fuck back inside — the doctor won't be around until later."

This occured on a Saturday. He did see a doctor in the afternoon. The doctor gave him a paper cup full of aspirin — about ten — which he swallowed all at once. Afterward he set fire to the paper cup, holding it straight out in front of 155 him, staring intently at the flame, half smiling, mumbling something in Spanish, until the flame burned his fingers and he dropped the charred remains of the cup on the floor while the smile left his face and was replaced by a look of sadness. Other prisoners had gathered around him sort of watching him in awe, talking among themselves, suggesting he was crazy.

On Sunday he remained alone in a corner, once again doubled up in a tight knot, sitting on the floor resting his head on his knees. Several Spanish speaking prisoners tried talking with him but he wouldn't answer. Or he would look at them out of tear filled eyes saying "I'm sick. I'm sick." Once the guard came down and spoke to him. He just looked at him not answering, until the guard walked away. Late in the afternoon, just before lock-up, he shit and pissed all over himself. His cellmate refused to go into the cell with him until the guard ordered a couple of prisoners to take him up to the shower and wash the stink off him. They put him under an ice cold shower. He stood there with his hands hanging at his sides, crying. His flesh hung on his body, exposing each bone. They let him out and he groped his way back to the cell where he fell exhausted on his bunk, his whole being wracked by sobbing. That night he kept everyone awake — calling for God.

Monday to Friday is always busy because the prisoners have to make court appearances. On this particular Monday, Alvarez's cellmate had to appear in court during the afternoon session. He was late returning so that we were all locked in for the night when he got back. He came walking down the line of cells until he reached his own. Suddenly he yelled, "Jesus Christ! The guy is dead!"

Alvarez had died sitting up. When they opened the cell and carried him out to put him on the stretcher, they had to straighten him out. He had died all folded up, his hands and arms wrapped around his legs which were drawn up so that his head could rest on his arms. Once again he had shit and pissed on himself.

He was already dying when I first saw him.

CUBA

Cuba is what is known in present prison jargon as a peddler. He is a real hustler in the sense that if there is anything in the way of contraband to be obtained within the prison, such as eggs, meat, grease, winter overshoes, coats, shirts, tailor made pants, special hair preparations, after-shave lotions, etc., he is the man to see. When any new young boys or fags or potential broads appear on the scene, Cuba is the first to know and loses no time making contact.

When I met him he was serving out the last year of a 10-year sentence. He had been paroled on one occasion and deported back to Cuba. He refused to remain there and, through some manner or other, succeeded in returning to New York where he immediately became a dope pusher. He operated fairly effectively until he was caught and returned to prison.

I don't recall a great deal of his past history although I became friendly with him and he spent much of his time telling me of himself.

The first time I saw him, he was coming across the prison yard. It was summer and he was without a shirt. The entire upper part of his body was a mass of scars from the shoulders to the waist and, once seeing him in the shower, I noticed a continuation of these scars on his legs. He obtained these scars — which are like shrimp-pink colored welts — by lacerating himself on numerous occasions with razor blades. Whenever he becomes enraged or has a right or does something of which he is deeply ashamed, he slashes himself afterward. Just a short while before I left, he went into his cell after an episode in which he had beaten a man severely in a fight and had been punished with 60 days keep-lock (60 days which meant almost solitary confinement) and cut himself so that something like 172 stitches were required to staunch the flow of blood.

He is short of stature with a well proportioned body. He 157 is of light tan color with (other than scars) a smooth, almost delicate appearing skin quite free of chest hair and nearly beardless. He has pleasantly symmetrical facial features with a large brown mole on his left cheek. His eyes are a deep innocent brown. He wears, at all times, a thin gold chain with a large (nearly the size of a quarter) medallion given him by his mother, and a thin red silk cord with a tiny rose-shaped knot in it, of which he is quite secretive (refusing to explain and resenting having anyone touch it) around his neck.

He considers himself a great lover and is always in the midst of a passionate affair with one of his fellow inmates. He constantly speaks of the size and shape of everybody's ass and will exclaim in positive terms, "Man, I got to cop" each time he sees an ass which especially appeals to him. He goes to great lengths arranging meetings in the yard with his most recent desire and will entice them up to his court where he surreptitiously feels them all the time, trying to convince them that they should try and get a job in the messhall where he is working and that all he wants to do is kiss them on the ass. He will say "Man, I no want fuck you, just love you. Man, I like your ass. Come in the messhall. We have our own shower there. We turn steam on in shower; nobody see; I cop lots times that way. You let me love your ass, I jerk off." Sometimes he is successful and goes around beaming at everybody and telling his friends all about how this time he has a lover that really loves him and that this time he is not only going to kiss ass but he's going to get in. He keeps himself well supplied with cigarettes from peddling activities and sees to it that his current interest is never without smokes.

He is a very kind person and is always doing unexpected favors for people he likes. He gambles a great deal and if he wins, sometimes gives all his winnings away to people he knows haven't anything of their own.

About a week before I left the prison, someone turned a note in to the Principal Keeper about him. Just what it was supposed to have contained, no one was quite sure, but whatever it said apparently caused the P.K. to refer Cuba's name to the prison psychiatrist, who promptly called Cuba up for an interview and resulting in Cuba being sent over the wall to the State Hospital for the Insane.

When prisoners are transferred from the main prison to the State Hospital they are, if violent, placed in straight jackets (restraining jackets they call them) and if not violent, are handcuffed and ankle-shanked.

When we last saw Cuba he was being literally dragged into the waiting station wagon and was wearing a restraining jacket.

COURTROOM SCENE

The morning following my miraculous escape (in a manner of speaking) from the shackles of the Law which was certainly one of my strangest and more interesting experiences with jail and the N. Y. City courts, finds me inwardly glowing because of simply being in the outside world. Also, this follows one of my most intense periods of self-negation and despair. Made of other stuff, I would have managed to hang myself, cut my wrists, end this involvement with life, escape into peace and oblivion. Never have I felt quite as alone or as unbelievably unhappy.

On Thursday afternoon, a hot and humid July day of last week, I cut from the pad intending to try at least to cop one bag of schmeck in order to turn myself and Florence on. Florence had acquired enough bread and we both agreed it would be fine getting straight. I had thrown my clothes on after lying inert and sweaty for many hours in bed, at about three o'clock in the afternoon, and made it sluggishly over to Third Avenue and Eighth Street, up Third Avenue to Twelfth Street in front of a Barber College where I met a chick of a few years acquaintance that I hadn't seen for quite some time, sitting on a sort of stone ledge in front of the Barber College with a newspaper folded back to the crossword puzzle and a yellow pencil that she was using to fill in the letters in the puzzle. My eyes had been alert coming up the Avenue and I hadn't spotted any possible people to cop from. As I approached, we spotted and greeted one another. The chick's name is Carol and she is a rather sad and beautiful woman of about 35 years of age who has had many wild and furious experiences knocking around in and out of the underworld. She's probably a good thief, has been a prostitute, a singer, a general hard type with prevalent lesbian-like qualities, but also likes and makes it with men. She is a trifle on the heavy side in body and looks well in slacks and tailored skirts. There is a small tattoo just above her wrist on the right arm. Her facial features are strong and, to some degree, what is referred to as "coarse." Her nose is inclined to be sharp and her sad and cold brown eyes are set rather close together. She is a mixture of masculine and feminine characteristics. Her hair is straight and is naturally dark, which she dyes a blond-red and keeps cut short and brushed or combed not severely but suggestively man-style. She had been using drugs in all variations for many years.

I sat down beside her and asked "What's been happening? I haven't seen you since last fall. Are you straight?" And then looking directly at her, it wasn't difficult to see she was obviously on, and I said "Baby you look straight." We spoke generally of a couple of mutual acquaintances, complained a bit about how hot the streets are these days with bulls everywhere, talked about a cat we both know serving time over on Rikers Island who had tried to hang up. I asked if she could help me cop and she said she had some shit — $3.50 bags — not dynamite, but decent. As she was speaking, she extended her hand over toward me, palm up and indicating that she wanted me to give her bread. I laid it in her hand and she fumbled around the waistband of her slacks for a moment, finally finding a little black tin box with a sliding top which she slid back and disclosed about seven bags inside, one of which she handed me. All this had been manipulated unobstrusively. I continued sitting a moment longer, holding the bag in my hand and was just about ready to arise and split when I became aware of a cat standing in front of us who addressed me, saying "Alright, open up your hand." He glared at me and, as I didn't open my hand as quickly as he desired, he spoke again, in threatening tones saying, "Don't drop it. If you do, I'll kick the shit out of you." I opened my hand and he snatched the bag. Meanwhile he had made remarks to Carol asking questions like "You got more. What are you — a pusher? You got works. Don't lie. I don't want to find anything more on you. All right, stand up. Hold hands and walk slowly down the street with me. Make a move to run and I'll shoot your ass off."

We arose as he bid and walked down the block with him to where his car was parked. I asked him not to make the pinch, explaining I had been out only a few weeks and that I was clean, please not to make it so I had to go back. Carol spoke to him also saying "Where's your partner? Give us a break. Wow, I'm going to be sick. I haven't gotten straight for the day yet. Can we get straight at the station. Where's my money. It's in that small black purse you took." He bantered with us, answering some of the questions and telling Carol not to worry, that he wasn't going to steal her money. He was sorry, he wasn't going to let us go. We had to get smart to ourselves. We arrived, by this time, at the car. He opened the car door, orderd me in back and let Carol sit next to him in front. We drove straight to the East 5th Street station house and were booked on charges of possession, and at 8:30 in the evening I was in the detention cell for the night.

Alone in the cell with the whole night ahead of me, I was ashamed and sure that many of my friends would at last call it quits. These people who had gone to the trouble and expense of getting me out six months earlier from my last bit — and here I was — not on the streets a month, and back in jail. Of course they would be disgusted. I wanted to kill myself. Thoughts of disgust, anger, frustration, confusion and a complete physical let-down had me exhausted. At one point I promised myself I'd do this bit and when I'd get out, I'd disappear down at the Bowery — anywhere — never show my face to my friends again, sort of fade into nothingness. What the hell; I'm old anyway. Fuck my writing. Fuck me. Fuck the world. Jail again — Motherfucker. Why? Why? Why? Actually, whose business but my own if I use drugs or poison? Is this the way it is going to be every time I move about the streets? Will some bastard cop, hungry to make a pinch and keep his record, show his boss what a great job he is doing and grab me and it's going to be here on in jail, jail, jail. Jail in the beginning was an experience and then gradually, through the years, became a sort of way of living for me which took up long periods of time. I was philosophical about it. I adjusted to it, accepted it as part of my routine. I didn't like it, but then this all went with my way of living and although I can still make it fairly easy, I'm now ready to stay clear. I don't steal any longer and I am not about to hurt someone, and now, let me alone to shoot my junk and

be happy with the people I have learned to love and have

faith in. Also, I want to continue writing, and one of the places I can't write is in jail. I simply dry up and that is it — no writing until I'm released again. Why in Goddamned hell can't they leave me alone. I owe them nothing. I've paid up my scores straight down the line. The scale should balance.

The night finally dragged into the daylight hours of morning. Somehow I had survived without going stark raving mad. I had asked the guard to call Erin for me and he had and had said she would see me in the courtroom in the morning. I had relaxed a little upon learning she would be there, and didn't feel as completely negative.

Saturday morning, Police Headquarters is busy with the first of the weekend business. The photo gallery and identification rooms start early, pulling the I.D. records and seeing that each new prisoner is photographed. All the City's precincts rush their overnight accumulated cases down early and Headquarters mills with prisoners and detectives, patrolmen and women police officers lining their cases up and getting through the preliminaries involved with proper procedure before the prisoner can be presented before a court and the case is legally court business. The "yellow sheets," as they are called (I suppose because they are of yellow color) are records of a prisoner's history as an offender, beginning with the first arrest and disposition of the case up to the last arrest and disposition of the case. They are thorough and complete, including every brush with the Law regardless of state, city or town, and, as in my record, date back in many instances to early childhood troubles. I have a yellow sheet four pages long; my record dates back to 1932.

Our bull, a man named Albono, who is a young and mean Italian type, had us through first. My photographs were the first to be taken, Carol's next and then over to the court building for the initial hearing.

When we were called into the courtroom from the detention pens where we had waited, a court attendant told me that Erin was there and had said she would arrange for a lawyer.

When we went before the judge where our cases were read into the court records, we requested an adjournment 163 until the 23rd of the month in order to have time to arrange getting counsel. The judge set bail of $2000 on Carol and $1500 on me. We were dismissed from the courtroom, returned inside and, after a short wait, were sent downstairs to be admitted to the Tombs to await our next court appearance. Carol, of course, was separated and held in the female section, until she was sent to the Women's House of Detention.

I was sent down with a group of twenty others to where we were relieved of our personal effects — keys, wallets, watches, papers, or anything we wished held in personal property until we could pick them up at the end of serving our time, if sentenced, or when leaving the court with a dismissal or suspended sentence, or when we could leave the Tombs no longer in their jurisdiction. Money is also taken and one receives receipts for the property and money. The money can be spent at the rate of two dollars every weekday for commissary.

Next one is called by name and lined up in a back room facing shower stalls, told to strip down, to turn pockets inside out and to throw their clothing up on a table in front of them. An officer goes along from man to man, searching through the clothing. Seams are felt, shoes are tapped and shaken out, and after inspection, are pushed over toward one. Next, one is told to gather up their stuff, move on along, take a shower, not to put the clothing on until seen by the doctor.

All this follows a line. One is called into the doctor's office and told to stand in front of the doctor's desk. The doctor looks one over for scars, tattoos, needle tracks and general physical appearance. The doctor (if one is a drug addict) inquires about the period of time one has been using, how heavy the habit is and how one is feeling. He asks if one has had several diseases such as cancer, tuberculosis, hernia and several others. He fills out a blue medical report card and one is dismissed, told to get dressed, step through the next door and wait to be given a Tombs I.D. card, have a forefinger print taken and to sign their names on cards for the prison files.

I made the round and received my orange I.D. card and
saw I had been assigned to the fourth floor. This was

considered lucky since usually drug addicts all go straight to the 9th floor. It is, as a rule, overly crowded and can be one of the most unpleasant places to lay around waiting for trial. There are always sick junkies regurgitating all night long, sometimes screaming, who are thin and drawn, physically debilitated to the extent of having to draw on reserve strength when it is necessary to so much as walk across the length of the cell. When the floor is fully loaded, I have seen as many as four men assigned to a cell overnight. The cells were originally scaled for one man, and are not bad for two. But three and four make it impossible for anyone in the cell to move. There are only two bunks. The others sleep on the floor. All in all, it can be rough and miserable. This sort of thing seldom occurs on other floors, and a man who has once made the route considers himself getting a break if he misses the 9th.

I owe my luck to the doctor. I had explained I was not hooked and was feeling in good shape. He decided to assign me to the fourth floor.

When one reaches the floor one is assigned to, one is next assigned a cell and it becomes his home for as long as he remains unless he is transferred to another cell later for some reason or another.

There are four sections on each floor, designated alphabetically A, B, C, D, and two end sections, E and F.

As I have mentioned the cells were scaled to one man. But with crime on the upsurge and not enough jails, it became necessary to put an extra bunk in each cell and there are now two men to each cell.

I settled fairly well into the daily routine. Up early, when breakfast is brought to the cell. Dinner and supper are eaten in the recreation are and one gets one's own tray where it is filled from the chow wagon or carts sent each meal time to each floor. Next, the men going to court that day are usually allowed to take a shave. Men from the day before who were sentenced are to be transferred to the prison they will serve the sentence in — Rikers Island, Harts Island, Sing Sing, Elmira or wherever it happens they were sentenced. The first couple of morning hours are busy getting all the day's business lined up. The men ready for court or transfer and work assignments for the men who are serving 165 time and act as helpers mopping, wiping, sweeping, stacking blankets, passing out toilet paper and soap, washing the trays and pans and any and all odds and ends that may come up during the day.

There is a good deal of action during the week and the days can slip by rapidly. But on the weekend, nothing happens in the way of action; both Saturday and Sunday seem interminable.

There are periods of lock-out when one must come out of the cell and stay in a sort of recreation area. These periods are the same each day. During the week, first lock-out is about ten o'clock and lasts until around eleven or eleven-thirty. Then lock-in until one, and back out till four; in again till six thirty, out till eight. This schedule varies slightly on the weekend.

Somehow one can establish a pattern for daily existence.

All the week prior to the 23rd, most of my time was spent in a state of introspection and trying to find an answer for myself and what was happening to me. Nothing seemed very real and much of the so called reality I was aware of appeared to me made up of a dream-like quality. I was in a state of torpor, surrounded entirely by a fantastic nightmare. I kept searching for some kind of basic reasoning to, perhaps at the very least, assure me I wouldn't be sent away for longer than six months. I had heard of a multiple offender ruling where a judge can sentence a man to a penitentiary indefinite term, which means from one day to three years and I am, if nothing else, a multiple offender.

I developed a prayer system wherein I kept asking for God's help and, at one point, requested a miracle — something which would extricate me from my situation in such a way that I would walk out of the courtroom and back into my environment of friends and beloved city streets.

It happened. Before explaining, it must be understood that there was simply no way to avoid pleading guilty, and the least any judge could give me would be six months.

The 23rd I was in court, just having stepped in, looking around and half expecting to see a familiar face. There was no one. Apparently no one cared to represent me and a lawyer hadn't been found. I would have to request legal aid representation. I was called before the bench, made my request, and the judge ordered the case to be heard during afternoon court session.

The legal aid man approached me. I had been ordered to sit off to one side and, looking at me, he said "I have sympathy for sex cases and drug cases and draw the line at violence. I dislike violence." Meanwhile, he had seated himself next to me and was scanning through the wording of the charge. I explained briefly a little of my feelings of frustration and told him I wasn't hooked, that I had been released from my last sentence not quite a month back. He asked me several questions such as, did I have a bag of junk in my possession when arrested. What had I been doing since my release. What kind of work do I do. I answered his questions directly and honestly, admitting to the possession, telling him I am a writer and am editing and assembing my writing into book form, that I expected to have the material in the hands of the publisher by fall. He interrupted me, asking if I had a title for the book, had I ever had anything published and what it was about. I told him there was no title and that it was a collection of my notes and stories of places and people and of my use of drugs, the things I'd seen and done — a kind of journal. I told him of my few published things, their titles and publishers. He wrote a great deal of this down and then said, "You know, I think you're fairly well adjusted and you are in luck. This judge is intelligent and one who has compassion and understanding. Also, the D.A. is an erudite man and likes to read. I am going to see if I can get you a suspended sentence. This judge is probably the only man you would stand a chance with. Sit still; I'll be back. Now understand—it's a gamble." He was gone a short time. He told me he had spoken also with the arresting officer who promised he would not say anything to jeopardize the chance. He also said "You will have to make a little speech, loud and clear, a public statement about your writing and explain the purpose of your book is to have it act as a warning against using drugs and that you consider yourself an example of proof, a wasted life, jail at the age of fifty still standing in a courtroom, charged with narcotic possession." He said "I think you can do it." I wasn't sure whether or not I could deliver what he wanted but with crossed fingers and another silent plea for help, I'd damn sure try.

And that's it. I pleaded guilty. The judge studied my case history, all the formalities were fulfilled and before passing sentence asked me if I had anything to say. I made my statement and apparently delivered the goods since the judge passed sentence of six months — suspended — and I walked out of the courtroom.

It was an exhilarating experience and when I left the court building and started walking on the streets, my heart was glad and I felt a touch of youth again in my blood.

QUAGMIRE

In making the change over from my recent incarceration to my present sense of freedom, I have encountered several difficulties. The most frustrating has been the problem of clarifying my position regarding the voluntary report to the Department of Mental Hygiene. At the hearing for change of sentence or, specifically, suspension of executing my second six month term, the request was granted with proviso I report to a court designated hospital to be checked for drug addiction, the implication being (since I had already been in jail a matter of almost six months) there was little reason to believe any evidence of drug addiction exists. And it was therefore presumably only a matter of physical check up and I would be free of further responsibility to the court. All of this was couched in rather vague statements. I complied per instructions and was interviewed at Manhattan State Hospital, only to discover I am expected to undergo a three month period of physical and mental observation before the hospital would be willing to sign any statement regarding my either being still addicted or not. At this point, it appears I will have to enter the hospital in order to clear myself with the Law and not create further complications for those who have used their good names in my behalf.

The whole routine is ridiculous and somehow rather frightening. I am not at all sure of exactly what to expect. Also, the hospital is huge and cold and looks to be awaiting victims to swallow. It sits in a sort of concrete morass of twisting, turning ramps and overhead roadways. I have until next week to try and straighten the situation out. Meanwhile, I am uncomfortable and ill at ease.

I feel trapped and unable to escape. The hospital looms ahead of me like some ravenous monster waiting to eat me alive. I have and am given no opportunity of avoiding it unless I simply cut myself off from my whole means of remaining in touch with people I respect and consider friends.

My circumstances have me in a position where it is impossible to function without stealing. No hospital — no chance of legitimate employment. There will be a bench warrant issued by the courts and the first time my name comes to the attention of the authorities and they are able to locate me, I'll be arrested. It is possible I could remain indefinitely free of capture, but I would be aware constantly of the threat of being unexpectedly investigated and, where I stopped by the police, regardless of their original intention, as soon as they checked my record I would automatically be faced with a term in prison.

I am tempted to leave this area entirely and if I was fifteen or twenty years younger, there would be no question about it. I would go head for new places, hitchhike, ride freights—any way at all.

I have little resistance. There are no drugs available without becoming involved in a rat race. My few sources of amphetamine are undependable and I haven't any money to seek and try for other contacts. There is plenty around and not difficult to contact, but again, I'm too tired and indifferent to become interested and I know the grind of supporting a habit would be more than I am capable of in the way of effort and energy. Pot is everywhere but although I enjoy smoking it, it hardly replaces my preference (amphetamine) and also, again, there is the lack of money.

I am annoyed thinking of entering the hospital on my own volition. I almost vegetate now and after ninety days of their intensive therapy program, I should be in as negative a position as possible.

Several of my friends will and do expect me to do what they consider the sensible and ethical thing — to enter the hospital. I am sure several of those same people believe psychiatric help will be good for me and are firmly convinced it can do no harm. It happens I thoroughly disagree. I do not want any part of the program and at best, think it a complete waste of my time. If I must die a lingering death, I don't want it to include personality and behavior adjustments at the hands of bureaucratic psychologists and their cohorts, the do-good, social service, program conscious, specialized and conscientious psychiatrists. I am far too old and settled
170 in my ways for rehabilitation and have no desire to join or

slip into the so called society of present standards, nor to concede for one moment that it is other than maladjusted. What rankles most is the manipulative nature of the whole bureaucracy and the indifference to the invididual's wishes. If I take drugs, it is most certainly my business and if it is against the law and I am caught, that becomes my loss, and I must pay in their coin. But they have no right to force me into a position where I must submit to mental probing and investigation under the guise of what is best or right for me.

When I asked to have my case reviewed with a possible resentencing in view, I assuredly did not want a change in institutions or their purpose. Had I originally been recomended for a drug cure program at one of the hospitals, I would have offered but little complaint or resistance but for the judge and the courts to tie me up in a mental hygiene type project, supposedly out of kindness and humanitarian consideration is a bitter dose to swallow. I strongly resent anyone forcing me to accept something against my wishes — particularly where my good is involved.

I can already sense the gathering vultures.

FLORENCE

Florence's pad—evening. Florence just came in. She is looking well and a bit agitated, perhaps unsure, although I seldom apply insecurity as a measure of what to expect from one's behavior. She is a strangely beautiful woman. She is and has been good to me. I am not sure exactly what our combination is apt to produce. I have, way in back, a sense or perhaps an awareness of guilt, believing my behavior toward her has been tinged with selfishness and I have treated her unkindly.

She and I have been violent on many occasions. In one instance, I became dramatic; screaming at her, forcing her back into a corner, falling over a chair, yelling "I'll kill you — kill you. Shut the fuck up please — please stop" half choking her, half insane wondering how in hell I'd become involved with her in the first place. We both had habits and it had all started with bickering and complaining about trouble getting a hit. On other occasions I struck her. We yelled and argued; snide remarks, sarcasm, hate, general shit.

Florence is a very open and love giving person. She is extremely hip, having moved thru several wild and great scenes as far back as Charlie Parker early years in the city. She has been in touch with the jazz scene — digging music and musicians, active and swinging people, hustlers and knock around people. She likes living and has a direct way of accepting all experience. She is neither bitter nor hostile. She is a trifle reserved when meeting people, using a fairly hard set of so called ethical evaluations while growing accustomed to the person. Yet she is without illusion and regardless of the manner or sudden awareness of having picked the short end of a deal, or having become stuck with it, she takes it in stride and continues to know the person or people, explaining their seeming deceit or treachery rationally and with a kind of understanding.

She is cognizant of a basic truth within herself and she
172 tries living close to that awareness.

We lived together last year beginning about April. We met at Arnie's pad on Houston Street. She came in during a session of amphetamine and pot smoking among a group of manipulative people moving around mixing solutions, painting, searching among boxes and in corners, behind hangings, passing from room to room. She wanted to cop some horse and sounded on Arnie who in turn introduced us. She startled me a little and I began digging her surreptisiously wondering how she fell in and what she was doing getting straight. She didn't, in a sense, look like what one might unconsciously associate with schmeck. Arnie gave her stuff and asked me to hit her. While we were getting the hit, we talked briefly. She said she was anxious to get away from the scene, get back to her place. When we had finished, she thanked me and gave me a kind of running verbal patter about how easily I had given her a hit, what trouble she sometimes had and suggested maybe I stop by her place with Arnie. She departed and I was attracted to her and hoped perhaps I'd see her again.

Not long afterwards, Arnie and I were out walking and just sort of knocking around the streets and, being near 16th Street where she lived, we visited her. She was living in a small but oddly comfortable room and her actions were seemingly sure and had an air of being productive. She was charming and I felt she liked me. She invited us to have dinner with her the next evening; we planning of copping some shit, relaxing in her place and eating.

She has and has had for the past several years a great little companion and pet, a sharer of woes and love, a very wise and good poodle, who is definitely a personality and individualized and in all senses of the word — Florence's little dog. Florence named the little dog Pooka, explaining a pooka is a legendary little creature of one's own imaginings, sort of made to order, existing in Irish mythology. She and Pooka are inseperable and much of Florence's desire to be demonstrative and affectionate is directed toward Pooka.

The diner was fine. Florence is a good cook and doesn't let the physical effort required to organize a good meal and prepare it drag her; she can cook good things to eat. We all got high, laughing, talking, exchanging stories and ceasing, for the moment, to be weighed down with paranoia. We passed several hours and Arnie finally cut out alone. Florence talked with me about her loneliness and said she liked me and would like overcoming to some degree her aloneness in my company. I was lonely also and although I wasn't sure we would become or might become close, I liked her with a feeling of respect and enjoyed her considerate little overtures of affection. Florence took care of me and was unselfish, sharing everything with me and materially giving far more than I. She supplied money and I copped. We shared our junk equally. The time accumulated and Pooka, Florence and I drew closer.

We decided to move and Florence and I walked the hot July streets looking for a new spot. Florence was against moving to the lower east side. Florence and I both didn't want to be invaded by amphets heads. I simply didn't want the responsibility of having to be constantly on the alert, perhaps protecting our possesions (or at least Florence's.) Florence didn't want that kind of excitement. We confined our looking to the west side. With the help of an ad in the Village Voice, we located a small but great little place on 9th Avenue and 14th Street. Sneaking most everything out of Florence's old place to avoid paying the last week's rent, we became established after several trips carrying boxes and suitcases, odds and ends such as a plant of green leaves, dishes, pots and pans, a couple of lamps, a painting Arnie had done which he gave to me which was huge and square and filled with bright tempera tones of royal blue, yellow green, red, amber, of happy cartoon-like figures of St. George and the dragon, the five or seven headed Hydra, an active little angel hanging in the sky above the scene acting as a kind of referee or guardian type role. All the figures had wings and St. George carried a yellow sword. It took the entire night to complete the move.

Florence had had a bank account when we first met and after the account ran out and we were up tight for money, we would cash a phoney check against the account. Later, this became our only source of income and we both spent long daily conferences about cashing checks — who we could hit, whether we should write for ten or fifteen, twenty or thirty-five, figuring each possibility for all it could 174 offer. It took us no time to run through the local stores where either of us were know. Florence had a wider range than I, since almost all these places knew her only as a nice little lady who sometimes had to cash a check. We tried any and all leads. Our habits had increased and we were living comfortable. Florence received a weekly unemployment check that we used to pay rent, stock in grocers and cop three or four five dollar bags. Our connection was on the east side and the first thing we would do in the morning of the check delivery was to rush to the check cashing store, get the bread, grab a taxi and head to see our man and get straight.

Gradually we began cashing checks with close acquaintances and friends. Florence visited people she had known for years in Long Island, Astoria and Brooklyn, while I began calling on people I had met on a more conventional level. I burned several good friends. This through most of the summer. At one point we lost our connection — who had decided to pack everything in, kick his habit, get off the scene. We had been good customers and before leaving he arranged for us to meet a half load connection (a half load consisting of fifteen bags for twenty-five dollars.) Between us we averaged ten bags a day and we planned selling the rest.

We started, at this point, copping half loads everyday, finally copping as often as three or four times a day. I began getting customers and had a good business going. Still, we never managed as efficiently as was required and our lives became a steady grind of scheming and conniving, shooting more junk, finding fault in each other. We became careless about our dealings with people who knew our address and they came threatening and pounding on the door demanding money, promising to cut us, and get even. We were behind on rent and had to get out.

Florence got her weekly check and we sneaked out again. Clive and Erin helped us. We had acquired a great little black cat we named Mister, and we had Pooka. Somehow we managed to get out with clothes and a few odds and ends. We stayed with Erin and Clive a couple of days and then found a room on Tenth Street just off the Bowery or Third Avenue.

I had been in contact with an old colored junk pusher. 175

He was anxious to set up a business arrangement on the lower east side. We discussed plans and he agreed to paying a month's rent for Florence and I and himself and a little chick he was taking care of. His name was Charlie and he had been in the business a long time. He would supply the merchandise and I would handle the business.

We located a spot and we moved in. Our location was on Tenth Street near First Avenue. The pad was a sharp spot and we lived there from July — maybe August, until October. By late September, I had a good business going. We lived comfortably, shot all the junk we wanted (or at least we kept our habits going steadily without too much hassle.) Toward the beginning of October, Florence and I began having differences of opinion. It began with drugs, or at least, I became increasingly more annoyed and spoke nastily. Florence was irritated also and became more tense. My business sense is not keen and Florence complained of Charlie not coming through fairly. She was getting her check and buying food and copping extra bags from Charlie. She was disgusted and wanted to get out. She began using goof balls and getting completely stoned. Much of her frustration was directed at me and I became unpleasant. Either Clive offered his place on Avenue A and 12th Street or Florence asked him if she could stay there. She moved her things out. Then she called me to please bring over a bag and the works and please hit her because I knew how impossible it was for her to hit herself. I made the run, delivered the bag, cooked up the fix and hit her. She had taken several Doriden and when the stuff hit her she sort of zonked out. I shook her and made some kind of contact, asking if she had taken goof balls and she lied and said she hadn't. I couldn't get hung up with her at that point, going over each time she called and shooting her up, having her collapse, with doubt in mind about whether she had O.D.'d or not. She staggered over, Pooka by her side and stood in front of the building rocking back and forth, staggering away finally back to Avenue A. This all settled into a regular routine and then one afternoon she had convulsions. It was my first experience with a physical condition where there was violent muscular contortion, a stiffening of the body, quivering rigidity, gurgling, gasping breath, dribbling streams of saliva hanging from the lips, jerking straining black eyes, fear and confusion. I held her. I spoke with her. I pleaded with her, tried placing a silver spoon on her tongue — something about not swallowing her own tongue. I cradled her in my arms, trying every way to calm her and help her. I succeeded finally, partially bringing her round and she had another seizure, not as bad as the first nor as long. My own nerves began calming a little bit and I could function a bit more effectively.

The days passed somehow and things remained tense and uneasy. A cat burned me on the streets. Called me requesting four or six bags, arranged where to meet me and when I got there, there were two cats, one standing in the doorway. We passed him and I caught a glimpse of him at about the time the cat stuck a knife at me, coming on hard saying "Come on man — give me the shit. I don't want to fuck around — give it to me." I was carrying it in my hand and sort of passed it to him, trying to pull away and keep aware of the whole scene. There was no difficulty and as soon as he had the shit, they split. The cat in the doorway bounced out and cut past me joining his partner and they faded into the night as I returned to the pad. I discussed it with Charlie and he felt we had been lucky it hadn't happened sooner. It happened again about a week or week and a half later. Another pair of cats. They also beat me for a ten dollar bill.

One morning Charlie and I were just getting up — his chick had been gone a few weeks and Florence was off the scene. We were alone. Charlie was making a phone call and we were preparing to get organized for the morning fix. I was sitting on the edge of my bed, just having finished lighting a cigarette, when the apartment door was wrenched open and in walked two members of the narcotic squad. They had received a tip on Charlie and he was supposed to have sold to an agent on some earlier date. They were easy going enough, snooping around, making wise cracks, locating our stuff in the drawer — our works, finding a bag in my wallet and arresting me for possession. We were permitted to dress. Charlie explained we hadn't gotten straight and we would probably be getting sick and asked if they would let us cook up. They didn't let us cook up but instead gave 177 each of us a bag and when we got to the station house, we snorted. It held me together through the day.

They offered me a proposition concerning Avenue C and lining up pushers and helping them to clean up the avenue. They said they would arrange a bail of twenty-five dollars cash for me and I'd be on the streets that night. I agreed and was released and told to appear in court the following Wednesday.

As soon as I left the court building I headed for a place to cop. I copped and went up to the pad. I felt it would be wise to split. Many of my customers were still ringing the phone — some had copped other places and hadn't waited. I had no other connection than Charlie and he handled the bread and source of supply. I stayed two and a half days, uneasy and unable to get anything practical going. Florence had told me I could stay with her and I packed my cases and deposited them and myself with Florence. We talked of my kicking — I could use her technique. Taper off with goof balls. She would go and see her doctor, have him make out a prescription for fifty Doriden. I don't know if I believed I would kick my habit but at least I could cut down. I felt beat and defeated and agreed to her suggestion. We got everything in order, copped one more bag of heroin, did it up, downed two or three Doriden and I remember nothing more until I awakened in the emergency ward at Bellevue. I was bewilder-ed and knew nothing of how I had gotten there. They told me my wife was also in the hospital and that we had set fire to the mattress and probably would have a touch of smoke poisoning. The police had brought us in an ambulance.

I stayed in the hospital a week. Florence and I had a short visit. She had been examined and they wished to take X-rays. She was an ill woman probably in need of surgery. We kept indirectly in touch by way of attendants coming down from her floor, delivering packs of cigarettes. Mean-while, the day of trial arrived and passed without my hearing from the police. I felt sure they had been notified and my arresting detectives would be up there to pick me up. The next day I was released.

Erin came up and picked me up and took me to her place. Erin had some amphets which she kindly gave me. I did a lot of writing, sleeping, talking and staying straight with amphets. I had lost my horse habit but was weak and beat.

Something happened with me concerning Florence and the hospitals. When she called to ask why I hadn't visited her and to tell me of her pending operation, I was unable to respond and I accused her of dramatics and hurt her feelings until toward the end of our conversation she said "Fuck you Huncke" and after a short outburst of anger and hurt feelings she hung up.

Time passed and Erin and Clive wanted the privacy of their apartment. Thru circumstances, I ended up living with Noah and Paul on Third Street. Christmas came, New Year's and one day about eleven o'clock in the morning (I was alone — Noah and Paul were gone) there was a knock on the door. I asked who was there; a strange man's voice replied "do you know this woman — she says she lives here." I opened the door to find Florence swaying in front of me.

I looked at the man and said "I don't know her" (and shut the door in her face.) All was quiet for a few minutes while I stood beside the door, my mind in a whirlwind of thought, shame, rationalization, sadness and anger at Florence who was obviously goofed up on barbituates. She knocked again and I opened the door, rushed at her, shaking her and telling her to stay out of my life, I couldn't take her in, I had no real business being there myself. She argued with me. She fell, losing her glasses. She sat on the top step refusing to leave and I hit her, hissing at her to get out of the building away from me. She cowered on the step holding her arms and hands up around her head in protection and said "I'm going." Then she looked at me and yelled "You fool — you fool." I went into the pad and shut the door. Several neighbors had stepped out to see what had happened and they helped get her under way.

I thought of it all day and my mind remained conscious of it for a long time.

Events occurred — changes — another jail term for me and then back on the scene in June. I heard from friends Florence was around and looking well. We encountered each other on the street. She was the same Florence I first met — bright-eyed and forgiving and lonely.

She invited me to visit and stay with her. She tries to 179

make things comfortable. She has bounced back up on her feet. She wishes to share with me.

I sincerely love Florence. We have shared a strange companionship. She is my friend.

My behavior has been bad. Somehow I behave with Florence as I never have with anyone else.

I want only to be peaceful. I want to be free with her and never again become involved in violence.

I am relaxed and comfortable. Pooka is looking great and chases her ball, is petted, wags her tail, generally adjusts to the scene. She is affectionate, playful, a little bit naughty now and then but a little impish beauty.

Florence is sleeping. She arranged everything for me before lying down so that when I am ready for sleep all I'll find necessary to do is undress and fall into bed.

I'm here but it is really Florence's pad. It is bright and neat and fresh and white. It gives off a kind of sparkle and I am afraid my presence alone will serve to dim the light.

MENAGE A TROIS

There are certain people, that when thrown into direct contact with each other for any length of time, make the atmosphere and surroundings immediately around them become charged with an element of danger and evil. Forces exist sometimes threatening only one of the group or per chance everyone. When there are only three people involved and one of the three is a woman, it is usually she who is destined to suffer, to be, if necessary, the sacrifice required to appease the Furies.

Two men and a woman. One man considerably older than the other — tired and weary to die, who sits brooding, withdrawn and confused and is no longer capable of actively maintaining his independence as to the manner of paying his way. He's dependent almost entirely upon the contributions of the other two for his food, the place he share with them in which they live and the doses of narcotics they give him, saved from their own which is as important to each as the air they breathe.

The young man is hooked and uses large quantities of heroin. He shoots up as frequently as possible throughout the day and he schemes and connives constantly, sparing no one in order to keep his supply going. He has lived on the streets almost all of his life and he knows all the tricks. He will steal from those he lives with as quickly as he will from strangers. Anyone he has met or who has taken him to their home is fair game and he has no friend he will not take from although there are several he holds to be close and prefers not to take from. He seldom tells the truth and bears love toward no one. He is alway lonely and is filled with resentment toward everyone. No one escapes his anger for long. He will change suddenly — from the affable companion to the menacing enemy because of a reply he doesn't quite grasp the meaning of and is immediately convinced he has been taken advantage of and he must have revenge. He has many people on his list of those he will someday cut 181 or knock the shit out of the next time he meets them. Most of his threats are meaningless and never become fact. He is certainly more than able to fulfill his threats and once or twice has hurt his victims rather badly. He is anxious for the older man to be removed from the scene as this would enable him to take over the entire front section of the apartment. The apartment is really too small for three people and it would be better if only he and the woman were to share the place. Of course in the beginning it hadn't seemed too bad since he hadn't realized how beat the other guy was and even then he hadn't suspected that the guy had lost his heart and simply couldn't make it. He remembered when he had been alright, had made it everyday and kept up a twenty-five to thirty dollar a day habit going strong.

BEWARE OF FALLEN ANGELS

I remember the scene fully, am able this instant to see both Elise and Bill vividly, their clothing, their faces, their posture, the particular area wherein the whole distance between them was almost split dead center — the essence of their individual selves meeting at that point and neither would give way. I remember the way of Elise's sitting and the way of Bill's half crouch, his left buttock resting on the heel of his left foot, the right leg bent downward at the knee, the foot flat on the floor, acting balance to myself to one side in a straight back chair — watching and listening.

The setting was strangely beautiful. There was a quality of the unreal about it as of a new dimension. Color was alive and glowing everywhere — reds deep hued and warm to faintest pink and flame — blues almost black and shaded thru pale to peacock — yellow, orange, green, violet, umber, mud tones and clear pure light. Huge squares of heavy drawing paper working on with blue and red ink, applied by brush in a seemingly casual manner rapidly by Bill who held chunks of a blue and red jungle from another world which filled the recesses of the front windows. Streamers a foot wide and of varying lengths from two feet to six feet of a parchment like material, containing one area after another of every conceivable color, shade and tone within which faces took shape before the eye, hung like Chinese banners here and there through the two rooms. A huge square of cloth stained in shades of violet and red, spots of palest green and larger sections of black, the center a large mandala, the rest moving out from it, animal shapes or Tibetan monks standing alone and in groups at prayer or worship, was stretched taut over one wall filling it nearly to capacity. Beneath it on the floor were two mattresses, one on top of the other, spread with an Indian patterned blanket of light and dark green and an afghan shawl in all colors. A set of shelves holding books sat between the two windows at the foot of the bed while along the wall opposite the hanging, 183 all remained bare but for a small handcarved wooden chest — probably Italian workmanship, holding two or three brass bowls and trays and a photograph of Marcel Marceau in grease paint and dressed as a sort of harlequin. At the head of the bed beneath one end of the hanging, a large square shaped portable phonograph (capable of deep tonal and volume control) sat, a record of mid-eastern tea house songs on the turntable, the strange notes and increasing tempo electrifying the air with rhythmic vibrations. A brass Buddha sat upon a black wood block at one side of the opening between the two rooms. A thin veil of lavender gray smoke from a clay pot holding incense eddying upward wreathed the head. Next to the pot of incense were two bowls (one wooden, the other copper) containing rocks and colored stones, beads in all colors, several odd shaped gold plated figurines, chunks of wood, two or three strips of fur and several phial shaped bottles with frosted glass stoppers. A book on witchcraft and the Tibetan Book of the Dead had been placed alongside the bowls and the whole group of objects appeared like offerings upon an altar to a pagan God. It was here that Bill had stationed himself and, half crouching, his hands moving about constantly, reaching toward a bottle of ink the color he wanted at the moment, holding it for a moment before unstoppering it and setting it back on the floor, picking up his flute and placing it to his lips, blowing several sharp notes that cut into the sounds coming from the phonograph, lowering it from his mouth and twisting it in his fingers, touching light with his hand the bands of silver wire bound round the body of the flute just above the mouthpiece of a silver ring screwed or forced into the end, replacing it finally where it became another item among his work materials scattered in front of him. Brushes, pens, knives, scraps of wire, bottles bound in colored cloth with seals of sealing wax holding it in place, or silk thread wound round the necks, needles, scraps of paper and cloth, several squares of pastel hued suede folded and stacked, a few sheets of rice paper in process of receiving visual creation, all spread out so he could touch first one then the other or splash color on them or carefully execute a magic symbol in silver or gold paint or heavy black ink on 184 the surface. He was never still — always changing things.

He lit a black wax candle and, selecting a fair sized gray rock, dropped hot wax on the top and then set the candle in it, until it cooled, then moved it next to the Buddha almost behind him. The light from behind gave an effect of seemingly emanating from him, creating an aura of shimmering light around his head. Directly opposite him on the other side of the room stood a huge refrigerator with a large bowl of fruit on top. Periodically someone of the three of us would open the door of this monster in search of food or more often to open the freezer section to take out one of the three bottles of amphetamine solution Bill had placed there after mixing and dissolving it carefully in accordance with his almost ritualistic formula. He had always believed in order for amphetamine to be at best and had a prescribed way of preparing it — it should be allowed to freeze before it was used. I am inclined to accept his theory as I have never used amphetamine that gave me as much of a lift or was as much pleasure to take. Next to the refrigerator was a straight back chair with a profusion of clothing draped over the back and piled on the seat — coats, sweaters, scarves, shirts, gloves and a hat. A table, square in shape with an India print on a red background which was spread across the top and hanging down on all four sides almost to the floor, occupied the space next to the chair, the surface a conglomerate collection of cups, spoons, ashtrays, saucers, salt and pepper shakers, matches, cigarettes, burning candles. One was in a tall thin brass holder and another stuck in the top of a wine bottle; the sides thick with melted wax drippings. A book of poetry was opened and placed face down, here and there were spools of bright colored silk thread, a small pair of scissors, innumerable small containers of pins, needles and small objects of all kinds. At an angle facing the table yet able to observe the entire scene without changing position sat Elise — her long black hair loose and falling down her back to her waist, a faded blue shirt open at the throat pulled tight over her full breasts and blue jeans, without shoes, one leg stretched straight in front of her, the foot just reaching the edge of the table cover which she was idly playing with by moving her toes — the other leg was raised and the foot rested on the edge of the round basket-like chair. Occasionally she would bend her body forward and 185 rest her chin on her knee. She was smoking chain fashion, lighting each new cigarette in the corner of her mouth and letting it stay while she stroked her leg with her hand or perhaps searched through the stuff on the table for something she wanted at the moment. She was in a highly tense state and was angry with Bill. Now and then she would feel around beneath an orange colored cushion covering the seat of the chair in which we sat until she located a small envelope containing pot which she would bring out and pass it to me in order for me to roll a stick or joint. Immediately above her head on the wall hung a large Japanese print of some God of children — the composition done in delicate strokes of the artist's brush. On the same wall were two very delightful drawings done in watercolor by Lafcadio Orlovsky — one depicting a carnival scene and the other a sort of cubistic pattern of triangular color forms. Across from her, I sat with my back to the door, separated from Bill by a desk stacked with books, papers, portfolios, pencils, pens, a letter opener, paper clips, scotchtape, paste and glue, notebooks, letters opened and unopened and a red clay flower pot in which grew a tall avocado plant rather gracefully — the stem bare of leaves except near the top where there existed only a few but a sufficient number to cause a bending of the stem in such a way it appeared to resemble the pose of a dancer.

We all three had been together without interruption for at least five hours and it was now well into the early hours of morning. A strange sense of the mystical lay like a patina over the essence of our efforts to communicate. We were aware of each other separately yet always collectively in a manner of telepathic consciousness. The very air seemed vibrant with electrical particles. Two related and at the same time divergent viewpoints had become focal centers for energetic discharges of thought. In some instances, they were assembled with minute attention to detail and balance of rationalization and frequency unleashed at the instant of conception. Bill believed in the power of magic and of the Phoenix Bird always arising from the holocaust of flaming destruction — thusly did God accept all things, including the dark forces and saint or sinner, devil or angel were the same. Buddha could lead one closer to the God force than anything known by western concept. Sweetness, delicacy, innocence, girl and boy, poetry, home and personal possessions were abhorrent and to be sacrificed to action and creativeness and if all crumbled around one, leaving them exposed, torn, hungry, homeless, then this was a cleansing and setting free and it meant nothing. One imagined personal suffering and should be glad of the opportunity to aid creativity. Magic was his tool and he would use it to help him create and no matter who or what was destroyed in the process. Elise held other beliefs to be true and strongly resented the evil she felt was the very life blood of Bill. She refused to see him, to look at his work, accept the magic with trust and did not believe it to be true. At best, he was a charlatan and unworthy of respect. Hers was a God of wrath and there were saints and sinners, devils and angels and they were all around us. She was a Jew and no one other than a Jew could understand her. There was no meeting of mind, spiritually or physically being possible between them. His words meant nothing — he used them only to try casting a spell. He wished only to bring harm and pain; his desires were base and smacked of the bestial. She loathed him and wanted him to leave. He was only a dabbler and as for beauty in his work, she could not see it, finding it irritating and vulgar. She did not fear his power and she had no desire to use his amphetamine because it was an evil drug destined to cause a knife between the ribs as a final result of steady use between any two or, for that matter, group of people. He might mix his solutions so they became crystal clear, pour them into bottles of pale blue, lavender or green, clear glass or frosted drop as many pebbles and precious stones to rest at the bottom as he chose; it was not a magic elixir. She moved about in the chair; both legs rested on the floor. Her hands were clasped in front of her, the elbows of her arms resting on her knees, her face turning full gaze upon Bill, a swift glance towards me and then darting here and there around the scene, then back to Bill and her eyes brown and sad and burning.

Bill returned her look for a moment and then began moving objects within reach from one place to another, his head twisting side to side and eyes darting about. Finally he picked up his flute and began blowing several test notes, 187 his fingers moving and pressing over the openings of the sound or note control locations suddenly hitting a sharp angry tone — blasting it out; it was shrill and piercing, full of complaint, almost hate. He stood up and reached for the refrigerator door, opened it, reached in and removed a dark blue bottle then turned around saying "I'm going to shoot up. Where are the works? I can't find my works." He put the bottle down on the floor as he started moving around, here and then into the next room, poking behind the books, feeling along the edge of the mattresses, rounding suddenly and pawing around the back of the chest. He pushed the bowl aside, lifting the Marceau photograph and muttering under his breath, saying once out loud "There's something wrong. Somebody is against me — where are my works? I put them down and they aren't where I put them" and glared toward the wall, shifting to the Buddha, at me, at Elise, at the table top, the desk, the floor. He gradually paced across the full length of the two rooms, stopping in front of the stack of suede pieces, reached down and there were the works. He removed the stopper of the blue bottle, squeezed the pacifier on the end of his dropper sending air and drawing it back thru the needle and satisfied all was in working order. He squeezed once again and holding it compressed, set the end with needle down into the bottle and let go. Slowly the crystal clear amphetamine solution filled the dropped until, when a little more than three quarters full, Bill removed it and after holding it a minute, looked at me and said, "you want it first?" I had been waiting to take off again — not because I was down — but because I wanted to try and get higher and wanted to shoot up as soon as possible. I reached for the fix, dug out a square red bandana from a pocket, twisted it into a sort of rolled length and wrapped it around my arm as a tie or tourniquet. I tucked the end in so it would hold and, holding my arm up, looked for a spot to hit. My veins have never collapsed permanently and although there is scar tissue over the areas of my tracks, I still have all kinds of spots I can hit without difficulty. I closed my fist, opened it, closed it several times and the veins of my arm stood out plainly. I picked one in the center of my forearm, rested and adjusted my elbow until I obtained a balance and then, hovering the point over the spot, began pressing and tapping it into the skin and toward the vein — touching it and (with good luck) the vein had been penetrated. Blood seeped up into the needle, into the dropper forcing the solution to slowly rise. I was satisfied I had made a hit and again squeezing the top, sent the blood back and the amphets into the vein. I felt it almost instantly — the rush to head like a short circuit. My body began to pulsate or grow tiny antennae all quivering in anticipation. My aliveness took on new substance and was alerted to the waves of energetic forces sweeping around me. My personal force developed an awareness and it was as though I would receive communication at telepathic level. The surroundings — already capable of absorbing force — drive, spirit and the flow of magic sensed, almost felt, never seen and only the results of utilization had been conducive to all the nuances. I was thoroughly elated. Finishing, briefly washing the works, I handed them to Bill. He went thru much the same procedure of drawing up the stuff — the tie up and the actual shooting. He could absorb a large amount at one time — mainline — and turn on in a flash. He started doing his work.

Elise had sat through the scene without comment. I asked her to turn on but she refused. She was playing with a handful of small items — two gold plated lead figures of Indian or Tibetan Gods, a neatly patterned brass wire ornament found in the street, several rings of silver and turquoise and Lapis Lazuli shaped or cut like an Egyptian scarab. Her eyes had become dream filled and when she emptied her hands in a lacquer tea box, the many small trinkets (stones, unset jewels and strange objects) sort of clattered into the box. The box was hers and she didn't want Bill to touch. He offered her a shot of amphetamine and she refused. She turned on once in a while; preferred doriden nembutal, seccies, any of the barbituates and most of all, heroin. She was stimulated by amphets but didn't like the agitation and storm within one's self she had to contend with and it was only seldom she would take amphets.

Elise and Janine were sharing the expenses of rent etc. on the apartment. Janine came and went as she desired. She spent most of her time with Peter and Allen but mostly with Peter. Peter and Allen were almost ready to sail for 189

India; there were three nights remaining and then they would be gone. Janine had met Bill and was fascinated. She had seen him once or twice previously — once taking off with him. This was three nights before Peter was to leave and supposedly they were together when, unexpectedly, the door swung open and in she walked. She smiled at everyone and said hello. She said "I'm going to see Peter later — he and Allen are visiting friends. I want a little amphetamine Bill please." Bill fixed a dropper and gave it to her. She turned to me, asking me if I would perform the task for her. I said yes.

Both Elise and myself were pleased with Janine's presence. Once I looked up to observe what seemed to me to be a rather speculative smile and glance on Bill's face as he allowed his eyes to rove over the scene and rest awhile on Janine. Perhaps in that moment he felt or knew they were doomed but had to come on, had to make a disgusting display of himself at complete cost of the night's opportunity, had to eventually make it an experience great and one to remember. Janine smiled toward Bill — sounding him in some way they rather had between them. Janine was genuinely touched by the genius of Bill. Yet she felt a deep sympathy toward him and a sadness because he was so at the mercy of people's whims as much as he held in contempt those not his supposed followers, refusing to concede even the slightest degree of his supposed freedom. His was a force both powerful and consuming and when it surged through his being, his face, his body and all physical aspects of himself became twisted and tortured, visible to the observer yet denied vehemently and in foulest language. His true beauty lay within, with perhaps only his eyes betraying that might be. Until he began creating, when his movements became fascinating to watch — his verbal outbursts, partially incantations that were melodious to the ear with an air of the mystic and magical and one could easily be caught in the spell until at the last, either one of his exquisite hangings lay open before, rich in color and design, or his paintings or carvings or whatever. And you knew, because you had seen with your own eyes, that these were not the result of contrived effort but instead had
190 sprung from the inner being leaping out through his finger

tips. Janine wanted to know him — to see him, to listen to him, to learn some at least of his magic. She opened to him and he responded — both naturally and with speculative forethought. He could certainly dig her if she was at all sensitive, and he was inclined to consider her a somewhat spoiled child hardly aware of anything but beauty to see; and then, she just might be able to set him up fairly permanently financially. He was aware enough of her circumstances to feel confident she was due to be completely free in a short time when Peter and Allen sailed for India. He had been attracted first by Elise — not only because of her strange beauty but also she was a challenge. Still, Janine was fantastically beautiful in many ways and he was sure she lacked strength and he could swallow her whole. He had failed to accept one very important feature of her personality — she simply could not lie. It was impossible for her to try. Nor was she in any way a conniver unless, (as it happened occasionally) she had to try and keep things going — that is — keep a place where he and his followers could work and ball. But in the beginning she still believed it possible to talk straight and be answered accordingly.

Sitting to one side, always stoned, my whole self was imbued with all happening around — the scene, the people and many many layers of consciousness just awakened. I watched Bill and Elise, Bill and Janine, Elise, Janine, Bill — and I was unable to understand the overwhelming goodness and the almost devastating evidence of possible evil. Ethically speaking, it was my responsibility to remove or at least try and remove Bill from the premises. Elise did not want him there. Elise and Janine had been sharing the apartment and Bill was obviously a threat to so neat an arrangement. Elise surely loved Janine and, regardless of circumstances, did not want to see her harmed. Of course some of the statements about a sorry end etc. were (even were they to happen) hardly worth the mentioning. And also (which is of utmost importance) she had absolutely no right to interfere — at least till such time Janine called for help. And even then, there is the problem of who has any right to try and alter deliberately what is with any two people. True, it is unpleasant to see a woman knocked down, her eyes blackened and so forth but in most cases, I've discovered that 191 the woman is as guilty as the man. Elise — beautiful Elise — knew it was pointless speaking directly to Janine. Janine would continue to do exactly according to her dictates.

I did not fear for her. Still, I did not want to run the risk of being alone — not because my loneliness bothers me, but mostly because I respected Janine's decisions, knowing full well that she had a clear picture of what she was searching for. And were I to come on as though I failed to believe in her, she would surely have withdrawn and in all probability, entirely.

Elise spoke to Janine, inquiring of Allen (who she truly loves) and Peter and suggesting Janine not take any amphets. Janine answered her question concerning Allen and Peter but told her it was none of her fucking business if she, Janine, shot up all the amphets in the world. She had taken most of her clothing off and tossed it in a heap, left the room for a small bathroom to one side of the room we were all in; she began filled the tub with water.

Things seemingly became a bit tenser. Elise shifted positions, spoke with Janine several times and maybe Bill. I'd rather drawn attention to myself, attempting to reach everyone at some point or another. Janine at some moment turned to me and half inquired, "amphetamine is good — isn't it Huncke." I am sure I didn't give her an honest answer, or maybe not dishonest; the truth being that statements and questions declare me as the authority, the undisputed one of knowledge so "he" must be accepted as having final say; this always leaves me in a quandary. Fuck it. I did mouth some kind of an answer. And besides, Janine liked amphets. Also, (and of some importance) she didn't want too much push from outside. She preferred her own means of obtaining her answers. She possessed curiosity concerning living and wanted to search on her own — I was honored she trusted me. At any rate, one goes back, in a sense, to the original plan of trying to tell a story and finishing in a concise ending.

I know Elise did not like Bill. That is not true — she was ambivalently attracted yet at the time of making a statement, it was of the evil lurking around. She was annoyed by Bill's interest in Janine and warned Janine that he would bring only harm. Janine did not concern her behavior with the result of what she was doing. Bill had claimed an awareness of magic, a familiarity with witchcraft — he could teach and prove his point.

Elise got up, walked over to the bed and flopped down. Charlie Parker was blowing. Bill had started another hanging. I had moved over to the table while Janine sat opposite in the chair Elise had vacated. She was waiting for the tub to fill. Bill joined us for a few minutes as we all three picked up on a jolt of amphets. We all enjoyed the action and Janine was interested in all happening around. Bill spoke with her and she seemed pleased and asked questions of her own. He answered by discussion and his creativeness; incantations (permitting observation) not recognizable as incantations, thinking perhaps there might be association of the idea magic, but certainly his only words were of his belief in magic. Janine watched and listened. The tub was full and she stepped behind the door, disrobed and sat in the tub, her movements and splashing audible. Bill put down his work and picked up his flute, walked over and stepped inside near Janine. I know little of their talk, their attitude toward each other or how they looked at one another but Bill taught Janine breathing exercises for long periods of sub-mersion in water — breath control. Toward the last, they called me in to join them. I heard Bill say to Janine "he has paranoia — he thinks I have hurt you." I was confused and at the same time it was of almost no significance. Any importance credited was a waste. It was debased of me to have feared for Janine or wonder about her actions. I went in and Janine was radiant — freshly bathed and still in the tub sitting modestly, her long blond hair let down. She looked at me a moment, her eyes huge and straining to see all she could, half smiling, momentarily drawing one hand thru the water and then back again; then speaking, said "sit down. Bill has been showing me breathing. You are not worried are you? How is Elise?"

Bill was squatting by the tub fingering his flute, a sort of half grin was on his face, filling his eye with Janine and making friendly acknowledgements of my being there.

There were two candles burning — one on top of a set of drawers that reached above the tub and the other stuck on the edge of the tub.

I sat a moment or two feeling all is well, it won't matter if I leave for a while. I spoke of probably going out — a walk maybe or simply to snoop about, maybe if lucky, cop a bag of pot. At any rate I'd cut by Jerry's and if I'd see him, all would be well — we could turn on. We had all been smoking off and on through the day and night — it would be great if we continued. We all three jived a few seconds and then I departed.

CAT AND HIS GIRL

Several years ago, when I was comparatively new on the scene involving most of the people I've come to know since then (and their activities) and when I was still unable to recognize or distinguish who comprised the hard core group from those similar to myself who had just fallen on the scene or had been part of it only a short while, I met a very beautiful young girl who, at the time, was one of the people I saw regularly. She was pretty obviously coupled with a cat whose reputation was of a questionable nature insofar as his relationship with woman was concerned and I recall distinctly wondering how it was anyone as apparently hardened as himself could find the patience to spend time with anyone as completely unskilled in the ways of living in his particular type of environment as the girl. I observed and watched both of them closely. It was soon evident that his interest was, at best, superficial and instead of possessing any deep regard for her, he held her in comtempt and was merely using her as a means of keeping himself in pocket money, since she always had money that she supposedly obtained from her parents and which she promptly turned over to him. They lived in my apartment for awhile and I got to know both of them.

Frequently he would disappear for a day or two at a time and she would sit around waiting for him to return, watching and listening to the innumerable other people who were either permanent residents of the place or who came and went constantly. Most of these people were engaged in some creative endeavor or another and possessed, in most instances, a full scale temperamental nature usually associated with the idea of the typical artist — which they seldom made an effort to curb or control and I remember thinking she was amazingly calm and seemingly undisturbed by the constant flare-ups of temper and erratic behavior of her acquaintances especially if, (as I suspected) she came from the ordinarily middle class background of present day society. Much of what was happening was certainly uncon- 195 ventional and extreme and I couldn't help but wonder at her not being obviously shocked. But if she was surprised ever, she succeeded effectively in keeping it to herself, never in my presence revealing the slightest degree of anything being other than what she had been accustomed to most of her life. Her personal conduct remained shy and unassuming, retaining always, evidence of nothing more than what one might expect from any ordinary, conventionally raised young girl.

Her appearance was striking mostly because of her very vivid coloring. Her facial features were very finely molded and impressed one with their delicacy of line. Her eyes were a deep rich brown — a trifle sad in expression. Her hair was a rich chestnut brown, slightly unruly and falling to her shoulders in length and accentuating the cameo quality of her face. Her skin was very pale except for her cheeks which were always slightly flushed and tinged with pink. Her mouth was full shaped and red. She seldom smiled but when she did, her whole face lit up and one felt one's self gladdened just seeing her. She was not very tall and although at first glance seemed thin, was in fact full figured with rather large breasts and well rounded hips. She had long legs beautifully shaped and was perhaps a bit vain about them because one of the few times I saw her lose her composure was when she discovered a run in her stocking and refused to leave until someone got her a new pair.

Occasionally we would find ourselves alone in the apartment and it was then I got to know her a little better and began taking a personal interest in her. Prior to the first time we talked together, I had accepted her along with the rest of the scene as charming to look at, but hardly anyone I might become more intimately involved with. There were any number of very beautiful girls around and besides, I didn't much care for the cat she was making it with and therefore, other than observing her, I had made no effort to get to know her.

The first time we spoke, we had been alone in the apartment about an hour and I was busy straightening and sorting a stack of drawings that someone had done and left in a pile and scattered about my room. She approached me hesitantly and asked me for a cigarette. I gave her one, extracting one from the package for myself and as I was lighting it, she leaned over and took a light also, then drew back and said "I think I like you. You don't seem mean and selfish like most of the others around here. Tell me, do you like Gore, the fellow I'm with?" I was a bit startled by her directness and since I didn't much care for Gore, hesitated a moment before replying. She noticed my hesitancy and spoke again, saying "I don't think you do like him. I've noticed you seldom speak to him." "No, I don't." I said "Frankly, I don't think I trust him — not that he has done anything to me personally — but somehow, there is something about the manner in which he speaks to people that makes me feel he is false." She sort of bobbed her head up and down in agreement while I was speaking and when I had finished she said "That is how I feel also. I don't know exactly how I became involved with him and I want to get away from him — but I like all these people and this place. It is a new experience for me. You see, my mother and father think I am insane. They have had me locked up twice. The last time, I ran away and they caught me and I had to go back and now I am out on probation. My parents hate me and I hate them and I am almost willing to do anything to get away from them. When I was twelve (I'm almost seventeen now) they caught me having sex with a neighbor boy and they raised a lot of hell. My mother said I was depraved and my father called me a whore and beat me and I fought him with a knife and he was cut. Now they don't leave me alone one minute and I have to sneak out of the house and when I do I stay for days and they look for me. They have reported me to the probation officer and when they catch me, I'll have to go into the hospital again. They give me money and sometimes I steal it from my mother's cash box or from my father's pockets. Gore wants money and I can't get him any right now. He said I should try turning tricks and maybe I will." She had said all this in a rush and sat looking at me as though she expected me to immediately solve all her problems. I was startled by her sudden outburst and her story had made me sad. There was nothing I could say or do to reassure her and perhaps help her. I did suggest she think about tricking a little 197 longer before trying it, telling her she should wait and that if she was going to do anything of that nature, she would be wiser to wait until she found someone else to make it with and that I was pretty sure Gore would only cause her pain and unhappiness.

After that, she remained around the place a few more days and then disappeared. I asked Gore about her and he said she was a dumb broad and had probably been sent back to the hospital and he hoped to fuck he'd never see her again.

Several months passed and one day, walking on Avenue C, I ran into her. She was looking very well and seemed glad to see me. We sat in a little restaurant and drank coffee and talked. She said she had gone back but was out again and had met some other cat who she liked and who she guessed like her although there wasn't love between them. She was happier than she had been. She said she had turned on junk several times and liked it. She had apparently managed to come to some agreement with her parents and she was now allowed more freedom of action. From then on, we would occasionally meet and she kept me posted concerning events in her life. Once or twice, she had obviously been straight on schmeck and once she asked me to cop for her. And then one day she met me and told me she had fallen in love. He was a spade cat and beautiful she said. I wished her well and said I'd like to meet the cat. We made arrangements to meet the next day.

I didn't see her again for almost six months and when I did, I was unprepared for the extreme change in her whole personality. She had grown sharp and somewhat hard. She had changed her hair style and was wearing more makeup. She said she was tricking regularly and doing very well. She had a habit and wanted me to cop for herself and her old man. I copped for her and we made a meet for later when she would have some more bread and I could cop for her again.

From then on, I saw her steadily and although I heard of her lover from others and from her, I never met him. Then again she disappeared and that was the last I saw of her until about six months ago. Again she was taking junk but this time alone. She and her old man had parted. She had grown visibly older and was seemingly reconciled to her loneliness.

Meanwhile, I had met her ex-lover. I had heard that he was a mean cat and had treated her badly, so I was a bit reluctant about developing his acquaintance. But gradually we became better acquainted. I liked him. He is quite handsome and has never given me cause to mistrust him. We have never become close friends but I have learned to respect him over many others.

We had never spoken for any length of time until the other night when he began speaking about how they had first met and how deeply in love he had fallen with her.

"You know man" he said "I really wanted to make a go of it with her. I guess it was mostly her family that messed us up. In the beginning, we both had jobs and were getting along great until her father discovered I am a negro. Man — he really came on at one point saying 'I know how to handle niggers.' He took her home and as soon as she could, she ran away and came back. From then on we stayed more or less in hiding. She had become disgusted and started going out on dates some girl she knew would arrange for her. She began making money and would come home sometimes with two and three hundred dollars. Whether you can believe this or not, I've always disliked the idea of a chick hustling or of my living off the bread she'd bring in. But at the time, there seemed nothing else to do. Anyway, our lives became hectic — we were using junk and twice she O.D.'d and I thought I'd lost her. We had managed to avoid her parents for awhile but they had hired detectives and one Sunday afternoon, they came in on us and she was dragged off home. Again, the same routine took place — she came back, we hid, she hustled and we shot junk. By this time, we were beginning to get on each other's nerves and our little affair was strictly on the skids. At one point, we though maybe if we could get married, we could still make it. I called her mother and father and made an appointment to see them. I kept the appointment and talked to them, asked them to let us get married. Her father almost had a stroke and swore he would see her dead before he'd allow her to marry any black assed son of a bitch. There was nothing to do but accept the situation as 199 it stood, but we both knew it was almost over. Finally one day, during one of the panics about two hours after she had left on her dates, I got a phone call from the Harlem Hospital! — she had been rushed to the emergency ward after being severly beaten and found unconscious but was doing all right and wanted me to come and pick her up. She had been worked over badly and her face was almost frightening to see. I took her home with me and during the four or five days of her recovering, we decided to call it quits. And that was that. Once in awhile, we run into each other and she is doing O.K. but somehow she has changed. She stays high most of the time and makes it first with one, then another. All she really wanted was love but I guess it is the one thing she is least apt to ever get."

I had listened to him quietly and when he was finished I could only think of how tragic the story was and of the vast amount of stupidity and cruelty inflicted on the two of them and of how little chance she ever had of discovering any kind of happiness.

WHITEY

I first saw Whitey sitting in his room in the hospital on the edge of his bed. We were both in the section of the hospital reserved for drug addicts who are taking a cure — or kicking their habits, if you prefer. Several floors have been set aside for drug addicted patients participating in what is referred to as Methadone withdrawal program, which doesn't necessarily bring about a permanent cure but certainly helps the patient cut down his habit, regain strength, and affords a period of rest almost invariably needed. As the cure progresses, one is tranferred from one floor to another in a sort of rotation progression.

I had just been transferred to the sixth floor and had been assigned a bed in a large room toward the end of the corridor leading to the gym and recreation room. A chance acquaintance from the third floor who had been transferred with me was walking alongside of me and as we passed a room along the way, he interrupted our conversation to call to a friend he spied lying on one of the beds. "Wait up Huncke, I want to speak to this good cat from the Bronx." We both entered the room and walked over toward the bed his friend occupied. As we approached, we were introduced all around and, wearing a smile which spread clear across his face with eyes full of a look of amusement, sat Whitey.

At the time, I didn't pay too much attention to him, although I had certainly observed the smile and felt a good openness about him. We didn't stay very long and went on about the business of locating our beds and making them up and settling in. My bed was located in a corner and I was fortunate in that there existed a certain feeling of privacy although the room was large and in a sense, wide open. From my bed I could observe the entire room comfortably.

Pat, a very beautiful young cat, had entered the hospital in order to cut down on his habit and fulfill a promise to his parole officer who had told him if he would take a cure, perhaps he could be reinstated; otherwise it would be necessary to return him to jail. He took an immediate liking to me 201 and while we lined up for evening snacks he had mentioned that perhaps his girl would come by with some hash and pot. He explained there was a way open for lowering a line from one of the windows. I hadn't paid close attention and later, when he called me aside to help, I was excited by the whole incident. Pat's girl came and we quickly lowered a line made of torn strips of sheet weighted on the end with a ping pong paddle out of the window. Fortunately there wasn't a bitch in the operation and drawing the line in, we were delighted to find a good sized package of pot and four chunks of hash. Two fellows had stood guard and there had been no difficulty. Still, there is no way to keep everyone from discovering some kind of action was taking place and several of the more alert younger cats were hanging around trying to find out what had come in.

Pat quickly made two packages of the lot — one of which he handed me under cover and told me to hold it. The other he handed to another of his friends, telling him to roll some joints.

That night everyone, or nearly everyone on that floor, turned on. We had all taken our sleeping medication and then drifted off into groups of three or four, out of the way of attendants and nurses and had smoked.

The result was one of the most incredible experiences I've ever had smoking pot. I walked around simply entranced by the scene of an entire floor of patients in a hospital, supposedly ill and run down — all laughing and talking and emanating an awareness of rapport and good feeling. It was great.

We were strolling around together talking. I was struck by the beauty and great openness of most of the people. Perhaps it was an unusual group of people simply come together under circumstance, but it was a remarkable gathering. All around me was an aura of sharpness and open friendliness. We passed or stopped and spoke with one after another of alert and aware young men. I felt alive and warm and friendly. My only discomfort was that of not being able to say some wise and knowing thing so that all of us could continue to rise above the emptiness and mean-inglessness of the world we are surrounded by, and my

guilt became intensified when I was addressed directly and

asked a question I was unable to answer honestly without fear of destroying perhaps self belief or hope and yet help eliminate falseness and guilt looking directly into clear cut and still trusting eyes. All any of those beautiful young men desired was peace and joy and the right to live in a healthy world.

We had passed Whitey's room several times and as we started past again Whitey walked up and joined us. He has good looking features and a certain quiet dignity of manner, heartening to encounter. As we continued talking and more or less taking stock of each other, I found myself relaxing in his presence and soon I was aware of a feeling of underlying goodness and was drawn to him like a magnet. Instinctively, I felt as though I had found a friend and my whole being seemed suffused in a deep felling of trust.

We all three had exchanged names and I said to him, "Would you like to smoke a joint?"

"Hey man — are you kidding?"

"No man, come on — let's cut down toward the showers at the other end and light up."

Pat, the third member of our threesome, decided not to join us.

Whitey and I smoked together and it was like a bargain was signed and sealed so that from then on we were no longer alone and we were each looking out for the other and what was good for one of us became good for the other.

Soon, I met many of his friends — mostly young Spanish American cats. We continued getting high and turning on as many as we could.

One of the most interesting happenings of each day's routine is the final time of medication when everyone lines up for their cup of sleeping medicine. I'm not sure exactly what it is made up of but this I do know: few can take it without getting strangely high — some stagger off to their beds, others sit around talking, trying to enjoy the last few minutes before hitting bed, in touch with one another, communicating and exchanging dreams and ideas openly and with a certain uninhibitedness induced through the sleeping draught.

The first night of our acquaintance with each other, 203

Whitey and I took our sleeping medication; then, taking a walk away from the central crowd of people, smoked a joint and the last of the hash together and decided to sit and talk on my bed. My corner had become a sort of meeting and gathering spot for some of the more swinging and active people on the scene. Several cats were singing softly in Spanish and a few were in a group next to my corner talking and laughing.

From one of the windows, one could see directly across the street into the apartment building on the opposite side. It was soon discovered that one of the chicks or women occupying an apartment directly within our range of vision was either completely aware of being observed or simply negligent about drawing her shades on the windows down and each night at least five or six cats were lined up taking in a scene of a woman alone in her room undressing and preparing for her night's rest. She was an extremely good looking woman of about 28 or 29 years of age whose body was an obvious delight to her and she seemingly enjoyed running her hands down over herself sort of massaging her hips, her buttocks and her legs. I imagine there was a mirror to one side of her room because frequently she would, before removing her last piece of clothing (usually pink panties) stand looking at herself, half fondling her breasts, occasionally bending slightly forward for closer inspection so that her posterior loomed out largely offering a beautiful view of her lower extremeties. She was a trifle on the heavy side and well rounded. At last she would either disappear into the bathroom, supposedly for last minute details of her nightly ritual, and when returning to view, would be wearing a nightgown. This happened almost every night of the week and it was certainly one of the happenings of each day's routine most popular with many of the cats who watched her nightly display and kept up a running account of each of her attributes, knowing her down to a large brown mole just below her left buttock.

Whitey lay across one end of my bed while I lay across the other. We had watched the disrobing scene and Whitey was making very amusing and entertaining remarks about her more prominent features. Gradually he grew drowsy — once apropos of nothing he interrupted himself and looked at me and said "Wow man—I feel beautiful." Finally he drifted off to sleep. I lay awake a long time, observing him occasionally in the shadowy night light, glad of his presence and comfortable in the closeness of his human contact.

Our boys on the next bed had dug up some hard boiled eggs left from the morning breakfast tray and offered me one which I accepted and ate. One of the cats said "Dig, man—Whitey is out cold." Finally almost everyone had settled down for the night. Two fellows on the other side of the room were still talking in undertone to each other, chain smoking and I watched the red glow of their cigarettes cut strange arabesques in the darkness. One of our friends from the next room cut over to me asking for a last minute cigarette and sat talking for a minute or two about junk and habit, people and places, at last departing for his own room. I too fell into a light sleep, awakening about 3:30 in the morning to discover Whitey still asleep, hardly having changed position. His presence was cheering and it was with some reluctance I shook him awake. As he awakened, he seemed amused to find himself not in his own bed. His face lit up in a big smile. He kind of mumbled sleepily about going to his own bed, finally getting up and as he departed he said "Goodnight, bro—good dreams."

Our smoke was gone and the next day we made plans for replenishing the supply. Our boy Pat who had made the first deal was still with us and he decided to pick up once more. Once again all went well and the next two days most of our crowd and several cats who were mutual friends although removed from the scene slightly—stayed fairly straight.

Whitey and I had become good friends and both of us had finally reached the end of our Methadone program. Both of us were becoming restless and bored. We had laughed about all the things we found funny and amusing in the immediate surroundings. This time when the smoke ran out our boy Pat had reached the end of what he could stand and decided to sign out. I talked like the proverbial dutch uncle to him about staying for a medical discharge but to no avail and that afternoon we watched him split.

After he left, Whitey looked at me and said "It would be great to cut out. Do you think you would go straight to the cooker man?" Then we both laughed as we realized the humor of the question and I answered him saying "What do you think? How about yourself?" He answered me saying "Could be — and then again maybe not."

That day I called Bob, a friend of mine who smokes pot continuously and asked him to bring me some, explaining the procedure — the whole idea he found somewhat intriguing. He told me to call him later and he'd let me know. I discussed with Whitey exactly what I felt I should tell Bob and mentioned Clive's name — filling him in to some extent on both their present setups and their origins. Whitey asked if they were close friends and suggested if they were perhaps Clive would be willing to accompany Bob and lend moral support. Later when I spoke with Clive, I asked him to call Bob and if willing to do so, tell him he would help make the delivery. He was most willing or at least sounded willing over the phone and later when I called Bob and told him Clive would join him, he became excited over the prospect of the whole adventure and we made final arrangements before hanging up. I immediately sought out Whitey who had gone to the gym and was hitting the punching bag when I reached him and explained in detail what had transpired conversationally. Whitey seemed pleased and we spoke briefly about making an effort to keep everything secret and turn on only our personal friends.

That night, once again both of us attained a beautiful degree of communicative contact and the hours rushed by.

The next morning I awoke feeling depressed and lying in bed, my eyes closed, I felt the limitations of my immediate surroundings and became involved with thoughts of the street, of what the future might produce, gradually becoming depressed at the idea of once again having to live alone and assume responsibility for my actions.

The depression became more intense and a cloud of despair seemed to hover above me. Finally no longer able to accept the sadness, I arose and sought out Whitey who also seemed preoccupied and who as I joined him, said "Man — let's split, sign out." For a moment I was startled — I had been thinking exactly the same thing. I hesitated a few moments and then looking at Whitey, asked him if he

had taken into consideration the ramifications and what

signing out would bring about in the way of an immediate change.

We sat talking, half selling each other the idea: finally Whitey raised his head, looked at me a moment and said "Fuck it man let's go and sign out." He began to move toward the counselor's office. A mutual friend, Tony, who had been asking us every five minutes if we had made up our minds to leave and what were we waiting for — why not get going, after all, we had bread if he had just five dollars he'd split fast and go directly to the cooker and get straight. Let things happen as they might — at least he'd turned on. He was a pleasant young cat of Spanish American parentage and he and Whitey had frequently sat talking in Spanish: occasionally when I had been with them, one or the other would interpret for me and next to Whitey I had learned to like him best of the innumerable cats on the scene.

At the moment he was laughing and describing in vivid detail what his next moves would be following his turning on — how his old lady would be right there and waiting for him to get straight and then make love and it was in the middle of his telling how he would hold her tenderly, pressing his whole body tightly against hers, allowing his hands to rove from the back of her neck down over her shoulders on down the center of her back when Whitey interrupted him, looking at me, saying "Let's go bro. You and me. We don't need any more cure or anything the hospital can offer. You say you have fifteen or twenty dollars and that's enough to get us feeling righteous and to buy a screwdriver. Man — I cracked ribs when I was ten for the first time and baby I'm good. Just before Christmas my old lady and I made plenty of bread and if you want to work with me, ye've got it made."

I listened to him, almost entranced watching his face and thinking about all he was saying and remembering another time when someone had made almost the same proposition and how great it had turned out and of how down I had been then and of how it had worked out like my being reborn and if this time it could possibly be as great and silently thanking God, lucky star and fate for again providing me with a friend who from all I'd been able to discover, liked me and was willing to accept an everyday association with me, become my partner and thereby give me a real reason for wanting to continue living.

Exactly as in the previous relationship upon our first becoming acquainted and without provocation — Whitey did what Johnny had done: he convinced me of his sincerity and then, looking me directly in the eye, had said "Man — I like you and want to be your friend" and my heart had responded and I had felt as though I had suddenly touched the source of a new supply of energy. Yet even then I hadn't thought much about future developments and now Whitey had just told me his wish was to be my friend, to share our daily existence together — just be together — let what might come, come and to hell with everything else. It was difficult for me to accept at first and then in a flash all doubt was gone and from then on, my entire purpose in everything I thought and did was for the two of us and all that meant anything at all to me was that I had a friend I could love and trust and that I no longer felt lonely.

Without further discussion, we signed out. The morning was extremely cold but when we stepped out onto the street, both of us were so full of good feeling, we were barely aware of the icy wind which was blowing in a constant rush through the city and as we walked along the street, out on the outer side of the parked automobiles in the street with traffic rushing by, searching for a taxi, sometimes walking backward, laughing, exclaiming to each other and to the surroundings at large about fresh air, the sun, how great just to be walking cursing because an empty cab failed to appear, laughing about how Clive and Bob had looked down below, seen from the window overlooking Second Avenue – observing the activity on the street and the long line of knotted strips of sheet dangling six stories down the front of the hospital and the two of them – Bob hiding in the telephone booth and Clive taking the opportunity of reaching for the line and attaching the pot or dropping it into the two thirds finished leather bag – Whitey had been making it, having gotten materials from the occupational therapy worker – and suggesting it be used for the end of the line both for weighing the line down and to make it easy for the man below and at last we caught a
cab after two and a half blocks and asked to be driven to

Eigth Street between B and C.

I could not think of anything in practical sense beyond the plans of the moment. I felt good. My steps were light and I moved easily and not like a man of 51 years. I felt ageless — neither young nor old. I felt sharp and as though my appearance was interesting and that I still retained what was referred to when I was younger as sex appeal. I looked at people and smiled and looked at Whitey, watched him and it seemed he also felt good and rather happy. We talked and rode along and made plans or simply dreamed aloud to each other of what was going to be. Of making a few stings, getting bread together, of Whitey contacting his man and connecting for weight in heroin and of pushing. Whitey had spoken of his old lady being up tight in jail of her owing the state time — seven years — and her having been popped out just before he had entered the hospital and her trying to beat her present charge and then maybe she would be reinstated and she would not have to go back and serve the seven years or any part of them and now he and I were making plans to include her — having a pad large enough for all three of us. Whitey had told me a couple of times that he was sure we would like each other. He had also mentioned his sons. He had two and they were living with his mother. He had called them every day while in the hospital.

Finally we reached Eighth Street and I tried to cop. The man was out and there was a note on his door saying he would be back the next day. I was embarrassed because I had assured Whitey there would be no problem about making a connection. From there we headed to another spot where we were again disappointed. I was beginning to feel stupid and annoyed. I wasn't absolutely sure I'd be able to find anyone else and it embarrassed me to ask Whitey to cut around the cold streets with me while I tried to locate someone else. Thinking to get him in out of the cold and have him wait for me, I stopped by Bob's pad and rang the bell. Bob wasn't home or refused to answer the bell and I had to continue dragging Whitey with me. He kept assuring me it didn't matter but I could see him shivering and I felt disgusted at the turn our luck was taking. At any rate we did run into someone who knew his way around and after about an hour and a half of knocking on doors, walking, asking people and covering a large section of the neighborhood, we scored.

I couldn't think of where we could get off. My works were stashed at Erin's and Clive's pad and I had called them on the phone and they didn't answer. I tried Bob's place again and he was home and answered his door this time. I asked him if he had works and he said "Yes, but they are up at Debbie's. I did a little schmeck with Debbie and Alex the other night and left them up there." I introduced Whitey with much enthusiasm and Bob was very pleasant and appeared to take an instant liking to Whitey. He suggested we try Debbie's to see if she was home and go up there and use the works if she didn't mind. I called her and she invited us to visit her. Finally we got off.

It wasn't the greatest shit we'd ever had but it got us straight.

Again, my old friends liked Whitey. Debbie and Alex were delighted with him. About then, we got in touch with Erin and Clive and they told us to drop by. On the way over, I tried sounding on Whitey about the people he had been meeting with me in order to try and discover his reactions to these new kinds of people for him. I was sure he had known few unconventional people and most of his friends and acquaintances fit neat and conventional patterns even though many of them were out of the ordinary because of being hustlers, junkies and neighborhood hipsters. The people he was meeting with me were a varied lot and the majority intellectuals and Bohemians. He had mentioned meeting a beatnik and since I detest the expression and don't understand it, I assured him there isn't such a creature but that there are a great many people who lead unusual lives in the everyday sense but that they were usually swingers and beautiful. He had liked everyone he'd met and fit into the scene perfectly. Erin and Clive were charming and Whitey opened to both of them.

Clive was annoyed with me and my irresponsibility. He thought the very least I should have done was stay for the three weeks cure and not blow welfare. I had been on welfare when I entered the hospital and if I had stayed for a medical release, welfare would have continued aiding me.

My signing out ahead automatically canceled out my case. I had taken all of that into consideration but somehow I didn't care. I had decided not to let it influence my behavior one way or another in the beginning when I'd entered the hospital long before even knowing Whitey existed and after our plans began developing, it didn't matter to me in the least. Once, hung up and disgusted, I had thought it would be better to go back to stealing than sticking around for welfare. I simply didn't want nor do I now want to be on welfare.

Erin didn't seem to mind or worry at the time as much as Clive, and she and Whitey and I got along splendidly. Whitey immediately liked Erin and Erin liked Whitey.

And so it went. Whitey and I cracked a crib over in the village and hit almost a blank. We were both disappointed but it didn't bother us. There were a couple of people who are kind and have been and they sent and gave me money and we lived and managed very well.

We rented a room for several days and when we did so we were both confident it would be only a matter of time until we hit a good sting.

Meanwhile, we scored two and three times each day for stuff and once or twice we went to bed stoned. When Whitey was feeling very good and he wanted to communicate with me, he'd say "Oh man — I feel good — I feel beautiful" and his face would be wreathed in a huge encompassing smile.

Everything remained at an even tenor with us and once or twice when the going was rough, I asked him if he wouldn't rather be home and he answered "No man — I like it here with you. We're friends man. This is it from now on we're together." I told him "You're the first cat in a long, long time — ever wanted to hang around with me. It's been a long time since I've had a partner. Baby — we've just got to make it — one good sting, just once and from there on it it will be boss."

The first weekend rolled around and with it came the winter storms. Saturday hung us up in the morning but the evening was great and we got high on everything in the books. But Sunday was a real drag — cold and miserable and began with both of us sick and no prospects of getting any money; nevertheless, we did manage to get straight and went to bed on one bag apiece with a morning fix for the next day.

The next day we again tried to get out and organized early in order to try our luck over in Hoboken. We never did get to Hoboken that day but we did get smashed on drugs. We smoked some excellent hashish, swallowed about four Seconal apiece and shot up three or four bags of horse.

That evening I was fortunate and got my hands on enough money to handle the evening comfortable and leave us with enough to operate without difficulty the following morning. That day and the days following proved to be fruitless. It seemed no matter what we set our efforts to, we were doomed to failure. Whitey didn't complain but anyone could tell he was disappointed and his patience was running out. I asked him several times if he was disappointed and each time he reassured me.

That evening, not having a place to go, we fell by Gail's pad where we were made welcome. Gail seemingly could accept the situation with her usual off the record manner and also rather liked Whitey, which made me feel very good as it did Whitey — so much so was more than anxious about where people were sleeping. She was charming and invited us to stay until we could get swinging.

We talked it over but held out hoping we would get straightened out soon and then invite her to stay with us. Whitey was rather smitten by her and I neither discouraged nor encouraged him, figuring that if they were to make it together, it would happen and all my suggestions at the time would fall short.

And so the week went — somehow — some way without any real setbacks or any real progressions and although each day produced its particular pleasure, we were none the less concerned with getting started and all our efforts were directed toward making money and getting ourselves set up.

We were pleased with each other and Whitey gave no indication he was other than satisfied with our arrangements. We could still laugh wholeheartedly and although we admitted our failures, we still believed it would work out.

212   Friday arrived and this was to be the day we were sure

to make at least a small sting and be set up for the weekend. It didn't work out that way and although we got by per stuff, the evening found us outside Gail's door asking if she would mind our making it at her pad a few days. She was very nice about the plan and we moved in.

Whitey and I spent the early evening with Gail, meeting some old friends who came by — Jake, Joel and Janine — beautiful Janine I hadn't seen in almost four years. She had been living and travelling in Europe and her lover had just died and she had come back home. She was even more beautiful than when she left and I was excited and happy seeing her.

When she was ready to leave, Jake and Whitey offered to escort her to her destination. Whitey turned to me just before departing, saying "I'll be back soon — five or ten minutes. I'm going to call the old man and lay some kind of a bullshit story on him for money." As he was talking, the thought flashed across my mind that he would never come back and I said to him "Be careful man — if you call your old man, that's it. Back you'll go to Brooklyn."

He kind of laughed and said "Don't be crazy — I'll be right back." And he swung out the door.

That was the last I saw of Whitey. He never came back and as far as I know never will.

AGAIN, THE HOSPITAL

Once again in process of entering the hospital, prayerfully hoping nothing goes amiss and that today winds up my efforts and by nightfall I'll be a registered patient. I am in all probability as desperately in need of medical care as I have ever been — physically run down and exhausted, my nerves frayed, my whole being tense and anxiety ridden and my body covered with sores and patches of flesh germ infested and ugly — particularly my face which appears misshapen and twisted due to large red splotches of infected skin, irritated from rubbing and squeezing because they were areas where (quite possibly due to a vitamin deficiency) intense itching developed and it became seemingly impossible to refrain from scratching and rubbing especially when upon close inspection in front of a mirror I discovered tiny black mites or specks infesting the sections of tingling and raw flesh and the slightest degree of pressure caused them to pop out to the surface. Also there was or at least seemed to be just below the surface a sort of network of channels containing black blood, unsightly and filthy appearing and it became a conviction in my mind that these channels were the breeding areas of the black creatures and it was necessary to merely break the outer layer of skin in order to rid myself of their unwelcome presence.

This condition of the skin is not new to me and even though in the past the results have been similar, I don't believe I have ever experienced anything to equal present conditions. Not only are the spots red and raw in appearance as well as swollen, but where the skin has broken, there are ragged lines of fluted and ruffled dry and dead greyish white skin.

I have gone many hours without sleep and it is reasonable to believe these sections are not only infected but contain torn and injured nerve ends as well.

The ordeal of having to face people while walking along the street is almost beyond endurance and accompanied by the awareness it is self-inflicted is so humiliating — at this point, I can only wish for death or that by some miracle or other I'll become invisible and pass through the crowds of people unnoticed.

Today is the third day I've spent trying to get into the hospital and if I don't make it today, I can't guess even what I'll do to get by until tomorrow. My habit continues to make the usual demands and I've run out of people who are in a position to help or are willing to do so. Allen claims to have run out of money and Panna has reached the end of her patience and there is no one else I can think of.

JOSEPH MARTINEZ

Joseph Martinez is a 24-year-old man from Brooklyn who was born in Puerto Rico. He is a drug addict and a thief. He is proud and full of vitality and a sensitive and fully wide awake young man. Recently while in the hospital, we met and became good friends. We first saw each other in the waiting room of the hospital on the morning of our admittance. We looked at each other and flirted a little with our eyes but we didn't speak to each other or become acquainted until later when we were upstairs and had settled down to the daily routine of our withdrawal program. We were waiting in line to pick up our last Methadone shot for first day. I had been in line ahead of him and after stepping up to the nurses' station and taking my shot (I use the word shot very loosely since what I mean is that I drank a small glass of Methadone — supposedly 15 milligrams) I turned away and looked directly into his eyes. He was three men behind me in the line and still looking at each other, I began easing past the men saying "How are you doing? Do you feel bad?" He answered, "What room are you in — I'll stop by as soon as I've copped and we can rap until time for sleeping medication."

I told him my room number and said "Boss baby — I'll expect you. I'm doing O.K. but it sure would be great to hit the cooker about now."

We both laughed and I continued on to my room where I stretched out on my bed and waited for him to show. My mind was full of curiosity and speculation. I had just started comparing him in my thoughts to Whitey when he came into the room with a big smile on his face and holding a couple of candy bars in his hand. He walked up and sat down on the edge of the bed, offering one of the candy bars to me; he said "You dig candy when you kick? I do, man — I can do up some candy when I kick. You look better already. Man, when I saw you downstairs, you looked wasted. What's that rash on your face? You take bombitas? My name is

Joe — in Spanish it is pronounced Jose — my full name is Joseph Martinez."

I liked him. There was something at once physical and of the essence of living and of energy and soul. His eyes were full of light and expression — communicating constantly and I imagined I could detect a glimmer of love and I opened up to him a little and soon we were beginning to know one another and he began telling me stories of his life — of his first love and he told me it with feeling and sensitivity.

Supposedly she was ten when he first made an approach toward her and he was fourteen. He spoke of her in tones of tenderness and always with a certain awareness of her physical being. It was almost the classic romantic love story of the shy and poor young Puerto Rican mountain boy in the city alone and on the defensive — part of the scene yet sure to prove his worth — when he would eventually fall by in his convertible, draped in a fine suit and wearing a neat sharp tie with one of those English collars (the very latest style) and a boss hat, the rim snapped down in front, sort of tilted a bit over one eye. Really looking good and a pocket full of money and then her parents won't object to him anymore or interfere with their seeing each other and of her putting down the man her family forced her into marrying and of course she respects her husband but her heart is for Joey. He said, "Me Joey Martinez — I'd show everybody. Huncke — everybody would see how sharp I am and not bad. I'd even go back to her church, although I've had a chance to see that's full of shit — also hypocritical — and I don't believe in their kind of God, if I believe in any. Anyway, her priest sold out to her old man because he kicks in steadily to the pot (fives, tens) attends the church functions. Naturally he could pat me on the back and tell me he understood and he'd speak with her father it would be wiser to send his daughter back home to the island, to Puerto Rico for a while. There were some wild scenes and one, Huncke, where I called them all punk mother fuckers and I held myself up tight to keep from smashing something over their heads, a chair — even the priest who kept trying to calm me not even letting me talk. And her punk father pulled her away from me, telling her I was a no good junkie, 217 a hoodlum, hanging around corners, probably out sticking people up and taking their money and using it to buy filthy dope to shoot into my arm, nodding and full of the stuff and I'd always be no good and should be in jail. We had talked about my quitting for good and I had almost made her the promise I'd stop if we could only go on seeing each other and her family wouldn't interfere and I'd gone to this church affair just to speak to her mother and father and ask them to let us see each other and I'd get a job and maybe he could help me and all hell broke loose when they had seen me walk through the door. It hurt me so much all I wanted to do was kill somebody. And I don't like to hurt people. I don't like fights and baby I can fight. Finally a cop came in who knows me and he calmed me down and he took me out with him and bought me a few shots at the bar, talking to me, telling me he saw things my way and they were all full of crap but I should remember nothing was worth going through all that kind of thing in the church and I should wait and maybe after I had lost my crazy feelings I should try and see her again and then talk to her people.

"I fucked everybody — I left him and went and saw some friend who turned me on and gave me sixty bags on consignment and I became a dealer and made a lot of money."

I had listened intently and had watched him — his movements, the hand gestures, the lifting of the head, the fierce expression in the eye when he had spoken of defending himself and the sly twinkle when he had spoken of some point where he had gotten the upper hand or when he had evolved some scheme and his slightly boastful tone when he had been clever or when someone else had pulled a cutey. I had known all along even though he was telling me a tragic experience and recognized all the fine points, he never failed to retain his sense of humor. I was pretty sure while he was enlightening me about himself he was still very aware of me and not a word or gesture of mine had gone unnoticed.

We became fairly steady companions and made a sort of comrade-like love scene — full of a sort of promise of becoming even more intense in the future. Frankly I was attracted by the idea but I wasn't at all sure I wanted things to take that turn between us. Joey wasn't Whitey. He had much the same interest but he wasn't as full of guile as Whitey and would be hurt easier than Whitey simply because he was already aware of loneliness in a manner Whitey had never been and therefore was more honest about his feelings.

He made me happy with his charm and brightness and I only wish I could do some beautiful thing for him.

Instead, I signed out, leaving him behind to remain for the medical discharge in order to meet the demand of his parole officer and fulfill the required behavior pattern; also he would receive welfare assistance. He didn't want me to split and I had to be unkind, but under the circumstances I had very little choice in the matter.

He asked me to meet him the morning of his release and I thought of doing so but unfortunately was unable to keep the appointment.

He would sometimes brag and point out his good looks, his form, his coloring and his great smile.

One thing he did tell me made him rather special. He had been speaking at length of his neighborhood, his junk habits and he told a couple of his capers and of the money and how he'd spent it and also of how he felt he was thought of in his neighborhood. He had been very open — showing no embarrassment at some of the revelations he at the same time thought needed qualifying and we were strolling down the corridor toward the nurses' station for the final medication of that day and he suddenly began telling me of a dream and of what message the dream had given him and looking at me he said "Nothing bad will ever happen to me because someone looks over me and takes care of me." I asked who he thought it was and he answered 'My guardian angel."

FANTASY

I asked Elise if she still have her notebooks and if she managed carefully. She said – my lord – I think it is time. They both grew intense and when the car in front moves forward we turn also up another deserted country – where I meet you – and we will continue as if this was the day of our last resort... You are now and for many. Most girls were staying all night and would be glad for a wild winter storm.

Tony put all he thought she could stand in the screw twist and nearly drowned everyone – I asked for my mixing bottle back and no one would as much as lift his hand to give it to me. I told you I will not be saved if all this fanfare dies down hard.

PHOTOS
by
LOUIS CARTWRIGHT

Allen & Huncke

Janine

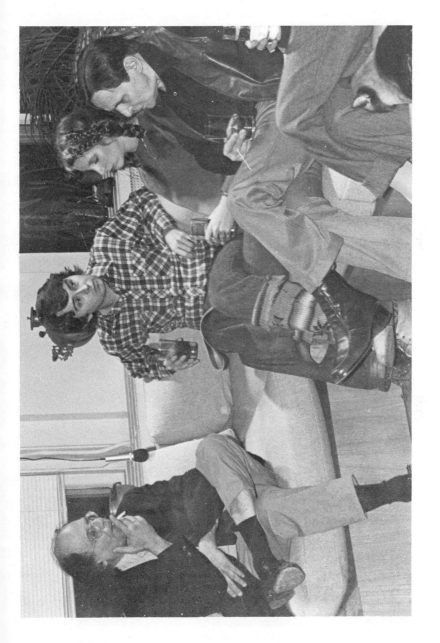

Allen. Charles DiFanti, L Fuhrman & Huncke

Bill Burroughs, Lucian Carr, Allen, John Giorno, Nanda & Huncke